BORN WILD
THE SOUL OF A HORSE

D1264425

Also by Joe Camp

The National Best Seller
The Soul of a Horse
Life Lessons from the Herd

Amazon # 1
Horses & Stress
*Eliminating the Root Cause
of Most Health, Hoof, & Behavior
Problems*

Amazon # 1
Why Relationship First Works
Why and How It Changes Everything

Amazon # 1
Beginning Ground Work
*Everything We've Learned About
Relationship and Leadership*

The Soul of a Horse Blogged
The Journey Continues

God Only Knows
Can You Trust Him with the Secret?

Horses Were Born To Be On Grass
*How We Discovered the Simple Truth About Grass, Sugar,
Equine Diet & Lifestyle*

Horses Without Grass
*How We Kept Six Horses Moving and Eating
Happily Healthily on 1.5 acres of Rocks and Dirt*

Why Our Horses Are Barefoot
*Everything We've Learned About the
Health and Happiness of the Hoof*

Training with Treats
*With Relationship and Basic Training
Locked In Treats Can Be an Excellent Way
to Enhance Good Communication*

BORN WILD
THE SOUL OF A HORSE

Joe Camp

14 HANDS PRESS

Copyright © 2011 by Joe Camp and Kathleen Camp

All rights reserved.

Published in the United States by 14 Hands Press,

an imprint of Camp Horse Camp, LLC

www.14handspress.com

Library of Congress Control Number 2013916405

Library of Congress subject headings

Camp, Joe

Born Wild / by Joe Camp

Horses, Wild Horses, Mustangs

Human-animal relationships, Horses-health, Horsemanship

The Soul of a Horse: Life Lessons from the Herd

ISBN 978-1-930681-50-7

First Edition

The Cover:

Miss Firestorm, conceived in the wild, born three days
after we brought her mustang mom home from a BLM adoption.

In this photograph she is four days old.

Photo by Kathleen Camp

*All of the links in this book are live links in the eBook editions available
at Amazon Kindle, Barnes & Noble Nook, and Apple iBooks, and all
photos are in color.*

*For every horse alive today
and all of those to come...*

*...and for every human who has never experienced
the wonder of being close to at least one of them.*

Did you know that every horse you have ever seen, or touched, or owned, or loved, was born wild? It's a scientific truth. Every horse on the planet is born with genetics designed over millions and millions of years to live and eat and roam just like those living in the wilds of the American west today. Why, I wondered, did I not know this? And does it make any difference?

Quite a bit, I discovered.

To the horse.

CONTENTS

FOREWORD

If something makes no sense, is not logical, the odds are it's not right. I learned this eons ago when I was told emphatically that a teacher wanted something done a specific way. I argued, because it didn't make sense for this particular teacher. It was out of pattern. Not logical. But the person doing the telling knew more about this teacher than I did. Or I surmised he should. It was his second year in the class.

He was wrong.

And therefore I was wrong.

And that's the day I discovered that, as much as I hated to make *any* mistakes at all, the ones I hated the most were the ones I could have avoided if I had listened to myself, to my inner logic, rather than to my friend. If I had done a little research. If I had just asked the teacher point blank.

From the day that particular teacher hammered me into the ground, I decided I would rather risk being wrong myself than actually *be* wrong because I listened to someone else when I knew better. Or could find out for sure.

Which brings me to all the folks we were listening to back when we first entered this wonderful world of horses. Those people telling us that the domestic horse and the horse in the wild were not even the same species anymore.

Not even close. *So don't go looking to the wild horses for clues as to how you take care of your domestic horses.*

For a while I listened.

But only for a while because I remembered that teacher. And started digging.

Our discoveries astounded us and in so many ways exhilarated us.

And that's what this book is all about.

PREFACE

I was terrified. My heart was pounding so hard I could actually hear it. Then suddenly there it was. A tiny foot. Then another.

Then a nostril.

It wriggled a bit as it confronted air for the first time.

It was coming out right side up. Just like it was supposed to. I mumbled a short prayer. *Thank you God.*

To this day I cannot remember the slime and the blood that I'm told had to be there. I only saw something gorgeous. A beautiful foal, on her way into my arms. Our first.

Kathleen and I had talked a lot about having a foal but had never stepped up to the plate. Forever afraid that something would go wrong. The vet would be out of town. Something.

But at last, here she was squirming her way out into life.

I rubbed her all over. Back, belly, head, tail. Poked my fingers in her ears, nose, mouth. Mama grumbled and stretched her neck up to look back at her work of art. She attempted a sniff and I scooched closer so she could reach her new baby.

Unlike puppies, or kittens, or humans, this baby would be on her feet within the first hour of her life. Eating and thinking and learning before the end of her second hour. Kicking up her heels and frolicking before the end of hour number three. And by hour number four this baby would be able to travel with the herd wherever it might need to go, which could cover as many as thirty miles in a single twenty-four hour day.

Except this baby wasn't in the wild. She lived with us.

And she would never have any idea how close she came to no life at all. Or at best an awful one. Perhaps even being sold to slaughter.

I thought about these things as I rubbed her tiny little nose, and tears trickled down my cheeks. Mama looked up at me and I thought: *She knows*. She knows her baby can look forward to a good life. A life lived as a horse. And I swear I could see, feel in her eyes, her gratitude. Such a moment I've never experienced before.

It was a moment I had dreamed of.

Literally.

Because that's not the way it happened at all.

BORN WILD
THE SOUL OF A HORSE

INTRODUCTION

The last book in the Old Testament of the Bible is named after the prophet Malachi. Pronounced like Sigma Chi where the *chi* sounds like the *ki* in *kite*. In Hebrew the word means *messenger,* and in the Book of Malachi the message is that change is coming.

The prophet Malachi intended to write a book about change.

In the beginning I didn't.

In fact I didn't intend to write a book at all. Kathleen and I were just trying to figure out how to keep and care for a small group of horses that had somehow landed quite unexpectedly in our front yard. We were asking a lot of questions and getting a lot of answers that didn't seem to make any sense. After stumbling through mistake after mistake, digging through an enormous amount of research, and spending a great deal of time with our little herd we discovered that either we were stark raving nuts or there was something very wrong in this world of horses. That's where *The Soul of a Horse* began.

Thankfully for us it turned out that we weren't nuts. At least not in the clinical sense.

And it was too late to turn back. We had little choice but to follow this journey and in truth it held great fascination for me as a storyteller. I've spent most of my life telling stories, usually involving animals, and here we were: two complete neophytes who, a few short months before, didn't have a horse... or a clue. Yet we were leaping face first into uncharted and very controversial waters on a collision course with the ultimate discovery that most "domestic" horses were being kept and cared for in a manner that is diametrically contradictory to their genetic design.

But even at that point, with that knowledge, I was not trying to create a book about change. It was a book about our mistakes, our astonishment at what we were finding, and how somewhere along the journey Kathleen and I both began to realize that what we were learning about relationships, leadership, persistence, and patience didn't apply just to horses.

That part was to come alive for some. Not a day goes by that we don't hear from readers telling us how the book has changed their lives. People who love horses and people who have never laid hands on a horse. This is all very humbling for us.

The book you hold in your hand is the continuation of our journey, the extension of our learning curve, and I suppose, once again, it will be called a book about change. Which is why we chose a very special name for our first-ever foal, the offspring of an unhandled pregnant mustang we adopted from the Bureau of Land Management. Considering the death sentence they were both living under - a sentence issued by our federal government – we feel the name is particularly appropriate.

So with all due apologies to my Cash, hero of the first book and author of its Introduction, this book will belong to new life on the planet. To Malachi... for all the reasons above, and to Noelle, Saffron, and Firestorm... for all the reasons in the pages that follow.

1

THE HERD

The golden stallion was pacing nervously. Something did not feel right. The matriarch of the herd felt it as well. They were both sniffing the breeze and scanning the horizon. There was nothing alarming in sight, just a sense. A sense developed over millions of years to assure survival for a prey species with no defenses whatsoever but to run. To take flight. It worked well or this herd wouldn't be here today. They would've been gone, extinct, thousands if not millions of years ago.

The stallion watched the wise old matriarch move around the herd waking those who were dozing and nudging those munching stubbles of grass. Telling all that they would be leaving soon. She was still fit, but getting on in age and slowing down. She would have to step down before long. The matriarch is the true leader of the herd, usually the wisest and most trusted mare. The one who decides when to move and when to stay. Where to eat and drink. When to sleep. The stallion is the protector. And the father.

There was a moment when the matriarch paused nose-to-nose with a young buckskin mare and they sniffed, and blew a greeting. Perhaps more. There was a special connection between these two. The buckskin was only seven years old but seemed much older and wiser than her years. The stallion had often watched her move through the herd, getting her way with little more than a look or a nudge. She was very confident and very curious, and had a funny little twist of her head whenever the stallion would do something she didn't understand. It reminded the big palomino of a special colt from years ago. His and the matriarch's. Maybe the matriarch had seen this as well.

Neither the stallion nor the matriarch knew why they were uneasy but they were and that meant *move on*. Predators are everywhere, often stalking the herd, waiting for an opportunity to isolate a young foal or an old or sick member of the herd. They were always around. Cougars, wolves… and recently man… and machines.

The matriarch knew where she would lead the herd. Many needed sleep. And her instinct told her they needed cover. There was only one stand of trees within reach, along the bank of a stream so the herd could drink as well.

She gazed at the big stallion for a long moment, then turned to leave. The herd followed, with no questions asked, and with no knowledge of the changes that were on the horizon.

2

A GOD THING

Why this obsession with wild horses?

It was all Cash's fault.

This sudden loss of my sanity.

But how can you not love Cash?

The day he came into my life he swept me off my feet. He was on the cover of *The Soul of a Horse* which is probably the reason it's a national best seller. One look into those big brown eyes and you're done. Toast. Everybody says so.

Yet all of this was clearly his fault.

Just a few short months ago had anyone suggested that we adopt a wild mustang I would've asked what the lunatic was smoking. We had a whopping total of three years experience with horses, none of them wild.

Wild as in horses who have never touched or willingly been touched by any human.

If such a suggestion had occurred my response would've been easy.

No.

As in not now, not ever.

God obviously knew this. And if you harbor the concept that God plays fair forget it.

He recruited Cash. The nicest, sweetest, brightest, most polite, gentlemanly horse I'd ever met. The horse who not only taught us how to have meaningful relationships with horses but with people as well. The huge guy on four legs who taught us more about leadership, patience, and persistence than any two-legged ever had. The dear friend who quite simply changed my life when he said to me of his own free choice, *I trust you.*

It all began with an odd phone call that sounded very much like a joke.

There was a family herd of thirty horses from an expensive bloodline that the caller wanted us to adopt. Immediately. All thirty of them.

I could only hear Kathleen's side of the conversation but her face told me something very weird was going on.

"No, I'm sorry. I don't care how valuable they are. We have no place to keep thirty horses. Nor could we afford to feed them."

There was a pause, then, "No we are not a non-profit."

"Are too," I whispered. That wasn't the intention of course. It's just the way it is in the horse world.

"Who told you that?" Kathleen asked into the phone.

I found out later that the caller had somehow made contact with a friend of Kathleen's mother who had told him that we knew everyone there was to know in the horse world. He should call us.

"Well Suzie is misinformed," Kathleen said.

Actually we did have a small network of friends with horsey ties, generated by emails and letters after publication of *The Soul of a Horse*. But Kathleen was convinced this guy was a kook. Who calls a complete stranger and offers her an entire herd of supposedly expensive horses, free for the taking, and wants it to happen now?

"No, really, I don't think we can help you," Kathleen said.

He asked her to write down his phone number. Finally she did, along with his name. And she hung up.

The man was looking for a tax write-off in exchange for giving the horses to a non-profit. The horses belonged to his wife who was now an invalid and could no longer care for them. They were being neglected because the man knew nothing whatsoever about horses. And he needed to move his wife to a place where she could get treatment.

"What kind of horses?" I asked.

"Polish Arabians."

The words caught in my throat. I tried to speak but couldn't.

"Polish Arabians?" I mouthed silently.

Kathleen's brow crinkled up in a knot.

"Am I missing something?"

"Cash is Polish Arabian," I squeaked. "Or is supposed to have Polish Arabian blood."

"And?"

"This guy is giving away thirty Cashes?"

"I don't think it works like that."

Kathleen was certain it all had to be some sort of scam. But I couldn't turn it loose.

Were all Polish Arabians of Cash's mindset, his personality? I was seriously bothered by the fact that thirty Cashes were being neglected. What if it wasn't a scam? What if the lives of these thirty horses were at stake?

"The man said there are twenty mares, most of them pregnant," Kathleen said, "and if he can't get a tax write-off he's going to sell them all at auction."

"What?!"

Selling at auction – not the high end fancy ones, the one's down at the local feedlots and fairgrounds – is usually for horses that can't be sold anywhere else and all too often this means a trip to slaughter houses in Mexico and Canada.

I went straight to the computer and sent an email with details and the man's phone number to everyone I knew who had any connection to horse rescue. Karen Everhart of Rainbow Meadows Rescue Sanctuary responded and said if the man would give her control over the herd she would see that they were all adopted out to good homes and she would run the adoptions through Rainbow Meadows so the man could get his tax write-off.

"Fantastic!" I said. "Wonderful."

Then a notion struck me.

I turned to Kathleen. "What would you think about adopting one of the pregnant mares?"

"We don't need another horse."

"I know."

"We can't afford another horse."

"I know."

"Much less two."

"I know. So what do you think?"

"I think I'm really angry at you," she said.

We're both beyond help. Even when we're late for an appointment, we'll pull over to the side of a road to watch a couple of foals romping in a pasture. We had talked about having a baby since the day we acquired our first mare. But fear of what could go wrong and our inexperience always talked us out of it.

But another Cash?

"Two Cashes," Kathleen grumbled.

"It would be a new learning experience."

"I know, I know," she sighed. "One that we know nothing about. One that we're afraid of. Yes I see where you're going. An interesting journey for the next book."

"Saving a mom and her foal from possible slaughter would be getting another good message out there."

"A whole raft of messages," Kathleen added. "Like why does anyone have thirty horses that they cannot afford to care for?"

I told Karen we'd take a pregnant mare.

Kathleen and I talked about it day and night.

"I wonder how far along she'll be?"

"How long is gestation?"

"I don't know"

"Me either."

Off to Google. And Amazon.

What a mistake that was. The first book to arrive was 279 pages long and only a few of those pages were devoted to how things were supposed to work when the new foal was born. The rest of the book went into graphic detail about all the things that *could, might, shouldn't* go wrong, and explained in some language other than English exactly what we were supposed to do about each one. The first instruction was to commit each symptom to memory along with precisely what to do should it occur.

I didn't get past the second chapter.

"Maybe we should rethink this," Kathleen said.

Our vet, Dr. Matt, assured me that 97% percent of all foalings were perfectly normal and should there be a problem he was not far away.

Kathleen began a list of all the things we were supposed to have on hand just for a normal foaling, then added the emergency stuff. The list would eventually grow to several pages.

I began to worry about how we would get the mare down to our place.

The herd was in northern California. We were in southern California. And I was, at best, still very inexperienced with our 25 foot horse trailer. Most trips were to the local park where we would trail ride, just a few miles away. I had almost no hours logged on freeways, and the longest trip I had ever taken was barely over a hundred miles right through the middle of Los Angeles traffic. I was a wreck. Do I make mountains out of molehills?

Absolutely, Kathleen would say.

Dr. Matt said a mare shouldn't travel during her last thirty days of pregnancy. Which meant that a vet up there would need to look at our choice, confirm pregnancy, and estimate delivery time. But the mare was not the only one who needed more than thirty days. We didn't have a clue about any of this and needed time to study.

We began to make preparations to fly up, meet the herd, and make a selection.

And I was dreaming about the baby to come.

It was always the same dream. I awoke one morning and wrote it all down. The birth of our new baby.

"It's beautiful," Kathleen said. Her eyes were moist. "I hope that's the way it happens. It's very sweet and should be in the book."

But the concept for a book and the recurring dream all vanished quite suddenly one morning.

Poof.

Gone.

The horse owner's husband told us that someone had volunteered to adopt the entire herd and keep them together as a family.

"How fantastic is that?" I said when I told Kathleen about the call.

"You don't sound very sincere," she said.

"Of course I am. If it's for real what could be better for the horses?"

"Right," she said, sounding no more sincere than I did.

The truth was we were both stunned. In our hearts we were happy for the herd. But we couldn't help missing that mom and baby we felt like we already knew and loved.

The baby I had seen born over and over again in my dreams. The baby I had already written about. The passage Kathleen had said should be in the book.

It is, by the way.

It's the Preface you read back at the beginning. The piece that's pure fiction. Just a dream. But clearly it served its purpose for I was now in the soup so to speak. I actually *wanted* that endangered pregnant mare. The concept was no longer a foreign thought. I was emotionally invested. The sanity line had been crossed. I had already written about it. And now I was desperate to see how it would all work out.

"It's Cash's fault," Kathleen chirped. "You got sucked in because of Cash."

It's true. If the herd had not been Polish Arabian none of this would've happened. I would've tried to find someone who could help the horses and that would've been that.

Someone other than me.

"Living proof," I said.

"Of what?"

"God doesn't play fair."

"Would you play fair if you had to deal with you?"

I glanced over to see if she was smiling.

I couldn't tell.

Our friend Cate Crismani had been following the story so I called her to pass along the herd's gain and our loss. She was strangely ecstatic.

"I love it," she blurted. "Now you can adopt a pregnant mustang instead."

"Excuse me," I said.

Cate publishes *True Cowboy* magazine which devotes many of its pages to the plight of the American mustang.

"A piece of our national heritage is at stake," she went on. "The Bureau of Land Management has over 33,000 gathered mustangs in holding pens around the country and now they're all under a death threat from the U.S. Government Accountability Office."

"Mustangs are wild," I said.

"You can handle it. And you can make a huge difference for a national icon. You need to do this."

"I don't think so," I mumbled. "Two new Cashes I could handle. Two wild mustangs are indeed something else."

"Do it. You won't be sorry."

I hung up with my head spinning.

I had studied the wild horse lifestyle for the first book. But I knew very little about the issues surrounding the federal government's management of the species. Or why they were involved at all. Much less why they had 33,000 captured mustangs in holding pens around the country (now 50,000!).

Back to Google.

It seems that most of the federal land allocated to the protection of wild horses in a 1971 law was subsequently leased to Ranchers to graze cattle and sheep. In violation of the 1971 law. The cattle and sheep were consuming the grass and water, leaving very little for the horses. So instead of removing the cattle and sheep, the federal government was reducing the wild horse herd sizes.

That made no sense. Surely I was missing something.

I found the 1971 law and read it.

I almost wish I hadn't.

The law clearly states that the land where these horses were living at the time (approximately 52 million acres of federal land) was to be *devoted principally* to wild free-roaming horses and burros. That means the wild horses and burros were to be the principal presence on that land. Not the exclusive presence but definitely the principal presence.

And on that land – *their* land by law – and *our* land, we the taxpayers - the horses and burros were outnumbered by cattle and sheep 150 to 1.

With a heavy sigh I pushed away from the computer and slumped back into my squeaky chair.. "Why me?" I wondered.

That night after dinner I dumped it all on Kathleen.

There was a long silence.

"Do you think this is smart?" she finally asked.

"Probably not."

"Are you up to the task?" she asked.

I had watched the likes of Monty Roberts and Pat Parelli do incredible work with mustangs but they each had thirty to forty times my experience with horses. Horses of every imaginable kind.

"I don't know," I answered. "I really don't know. But it could be important to try."

"It's definitely not going to be like training Cash."

"Copy that," I said.

"Then she'll be your Christmas present."

Our original entry into the horse world began with Kathleen giving me a trail ride for my birthday. Two weeks later we owned three horses. Now a pregnant mustang for Christmas. What, I wondered, might Fathers Day bring?

3

THE MACHINE

The roar was deafening. And very close.

Too close.

The matriarch fought her instinct to run. It was an ancient instinct developed over millions of years to keep her safe. And to keep the herd safe. But this time the matriarch knew that safety depended upon the cover of the trees. It was a foreign emotion to walk slowly among the herd, impassively, trying to keep them calm and together. But she had felt this pulsing thunder before, and had seen it. She knew what it was. So did the stallion.

The big palomino was searching the tops of the trees, trying to find the sound through the patchwork of limbs and leaves. It was getting louder. Closer. Every fiber in his body wanted to *run* but he remembered the last time. He remembered what could happen out in the open.

Suddenly there it was, right above them. Barely above the treetops. Whirling blades tearing at the tree limbs. There was much snorting and shuffling of feet but the matriarch and the stallion worked hard at keeping their own adrenaline at bay which helped the others.

The stallion had watched from high atop a rocky plateau as a machine like this had gotten behind another band from their herd and had driven them into a canyon surrounded by cliffs. Men appeared at the entrance and slammed metal walls blocking any escape. The stallion never saw any of this band again. The images racing through his memory were all filled with fear. Glassy eyes. Screams of anguish.

As the machine whirled off toward the setting sun the matriarch was already gathering her charges and moving them out of the trees in the opposite direction. The buckskin mare joined her at the head of the herd and broke their trot into a full gallop trying to put as much distance between them and the deafening noise as possible. She too knew what it could mean. Too well. The stallion brought up the rear. They ran, and ran, and ran.

It would be night soon and they would be safe. The matriarch was tiring but she kept pushing until she could run no more. Then she slept deeply, surrounded by her herd. The buckskin mare stood watch, the sentinel, scanning the distant horizons.

There was no sign of the machine. But the big golden stallion was still uneasy.

Nothing seemed to feel right anymore.

4

TO CIVILIZE

My first call to the Bureau of Land Management office in Reno had generated an entire photo album of pregnant mustangs, all living in a holding pen at the their adoption facility. We made several early selections and scheduled a flight to Reno to make a final decision.

"Why do I need to go," Kathleen groaned.

"You see things through different eyes than I do," I said. "And this *is* your Christmas present to me."

"God isn't the only one who doesn't play fair," she smiled.

"If we do in fact select one," I said, "when we go pick her up you *have* to drive up with me. It's a twelve-hour trip each way and pulling that big long trailer through the mountains in December terrifies me."

"I'm sure it does, Sweetie." She paused. "There's more isn't there?"

"What do you mean?"

"That's not all that terrifies you."

I hate it when she's perceptive.

"You're having second thoughts aren't you?"

Silence.

I had been asking a lot of questions since we had actually gone on record and scheduled the trip to Reno. Or more accurately, the same question, over and over.

What do domesticated horses and wild horses have in common?

I needed reassurance that I hadn't stepped in over my head.

The answer was always the same.

Nothing.

Nothing at all.

Emphatically delivered.

By virtually everybody.

We were told that wild horses and domesticated horses were like different species.

Why, I wondered.

Because they're... wild. Like a tiger or a cougar.

The word conjures that image doesn't it? We've all seen it in movies and photographs. A couple of stallions on their hind legs pawing and biting at each other. The word *wild* tends to connote vicious, mean, predatory behavior.

I was at the doctor's office for my annual physical and the subject of our plans to adopt a pregnant mustang came up.

"Will she bite and kick? How will you tame her?" he blurted right at the beginning.

So, yes, all this talk about *wild* was beginning to get to me.

Would I be up to it?

The Oxford English Dictionary definition of domesticate is: To tame or bring under control; to civilize.

To civilize?

Kathleen pulled up the bevy of photos sent to us by the BLM. Not one of them seemed to need *civilizing*.

"These don't look like vicious beasts," I said.

"Worried, maybe," Kathleen said. "Fearful, perhaps, but like most horses, probably very generous."

We talked about our reading of Pete and Ivy Ramey's trip into wild horse country. And what pray tell was not civilized about those horses? Did they kill living beings? Did they destroy things? Were they mean? To be feared? The answer, of course, was no to all of the above. And every day someone new is proving that the mustang who has lived his entire life in the wild can say yes to a relationship with humans when given the opportunity and treated with patience and compassion.

I was breathing easier. The trip to Reno was back on.

Deep down, I already knew that genetically there was no difference at all between the wild and domestic horses? So I shouldn't have been worried.

Shortly after our first three horses had shown up in our front yard I had stumbled into wild horse research trying to uncover why Cash had come to us with shoes on his front feet but none on his back feet. We had been told that concrete and asphalt would crack and shatter any horse's hoof that was not wearing a shoe. If that were true, I needed to get shoes on his back feet right now because we had concrete and asphalt everywhere.

And I suppose I had wondered – apparently too often too loudly – how wild horses had managed to exist all this time without help from humans? Could it be the wild ones might be able to teach us a thing or two?

Oh no. Generations of selective breeding have completely changed everything about the domesticated horse.

That's when I happened upon Jaime Jackson's research on how wild horse hooves work and look, and why. And how well their hooves had protected them and helped them survive for millions of years.

To a prey animal like a wild horse there is nothing more important than good rock-solid feet. They travel up to thirty miles a day in search of food and water. And they run a lot from predators.

Without metal shoes.

But folks wanted us to believe that was all immaterial. The wild horse and the domesticated horse were different species.

Everybody said so.

A few hundred years of selective breeding had made it so.

Domesticated horses no longer had the same feet as their wild counterparts.

A domesticated hoof was destined to be weak and underdeveloped. Often sick and unhealthy. A domesticated hoof needed a metal shoe.

The American Farriers Journal reported that 95% of all domesticated horses have some sort of lameness issue. That's why they have to wear shoes, I was told.

But Cash only had *two* shoes.

So was he half wild and half domesticated?

It was worrisome that his back end would be the wild part. The kicking end.

All of this was gnawing at the edges of logic.

There was virtually no hoof lameness in the wild. And it was rampant throughout the domestic scene.

But unlike everyone else we had encountered, Jaime Jackson believed that wild hoof mechanics were exactly the same as domesticated hoof mechanics, both depending upon the hoof to flex with every step taken. Like a toilet plunger. This flexing circulates an enormous amount of blood into the hoof capsule, and helps push it back up the leg. Like a mini-heart, pumping with every step. Among other things this keeps the hoof healthy and growing properly.

And what happens when a metal shoe is nailed to the hoof?

Nothing.

No flexing.

No blood.

No function.

The curtains were parting. A veil lifting. It wasn't about whether a horse was *domesticated* or *wild*. It was about blood circulation. And the effect of that circulation - or lack of it - on the health of the hoof.

No, no, no. We've unfortunately bred the foot right off the horse.

I smiled politely.

Knowledge is king.

I had just read an article in a scientific journal that stated it would take a minimum of 5000 years to even begin to change the base genetics of any species. Probably closer to

10,000, depending upon the circumstances. A few hundred years of selective breeding would have no affect whatsoever on base genetics.

Which is why a newborn foal will still be on his feet less than an hour after being born - thinking, learning, eating - and in less than four hours be ready and able to move out with the herd to stay away from predators. Even if he's born in a stall.

The genetics haven't changed.

It's also why the stresses, illnesses, and vices caused by being confined to a stall can be solved by allowing horses to be out with each other 24/7. And it's why barefoot "domestic" horses living out with a herd and eating a proper sugar-free diet from the ground are able to develop rock-solid hooves that have no use for metal shoes.

I called our vet.

"The shoes are coming off ," I said.

"Uhh… whose?"

"All of 'em."

Silence.

Then, "Why not try one at a time and see how it goes?"

"Nope. All six."

In a week it was done.

And not one of our horses ever looked back. I had never seen a horse smile until the day Cash's shoes were removed.

Scribbles, our paint, had hooves that were so sick that he had to grow a whole new foot, from hairline to the ground. It took eight months. But then he too was a happy camper.

How could this be?

Domesticated horses need shoes because their feet are sick, soft, and unhealthy. Or could it be that their feet are sick, soft, and unhealthy *because* of the metal shoes nailed to their feet restricting the circulation and eliminating the natural hydraulic-like shock absorption the blood provides to protect the joints, ligaments, and tendons of the leg? I guess that's why the folks who run one of the country's largest mounted police patrol units in Houston, Texas, have not one shoe on their forty or so horses who work all day every day on concrete, asphalt, and marble. Unfortunately I didn't know this at the time.

"Which means that wild and domestic horses are not two different species at all," Kathleen said. "They're the same."

"I could turn Cash out into the wild and he'd be fine," I said.

"Down boy. That's taking research a step too far." She wasn't smiling.

The American Association for the Advancement of Science says that every horse on the planet retains the ability to revert to living in the wild successfully.

DNA sequences taken from long bone remains of horses found preserved in the Alaskan permafrost dated 12,000 to 28,000 years ago differ by as little as 1.2% from the modern domestic horse. The horse in your back yard.

So genetically speaking there is really no difference between a horse living in the wild and a so-called domesticated horse. What each horse has learned from his or her environment is obviously different, as I would soon come to understand. But their genetic ability to live successfully in the wild is the same.

And there was good news in the realization.

We had in our care perhaps the only species on the planet that lives with humans but could boast its own living laboratory in the wild. No more need for guesswork. These wild horses could reveal the truth, be a road map to the way horses were designed to live. A way that works because they have survived for millions and millions of years.

God and Mother Nature knew what they were doing. Horses were designed over time through trial and error to live and eat and move in certain ways; and the study of all of this could provide more incredibly valuable information about how we should be feeding, keeping, and caring for the horses we choose to associate with than has ever been understood before.

So I was astonished when I learned that we were at risk of losing America's wild horses.

How could that be?

These horses are not only a living laboratory, as a group they are a legendary icon of the American west; sentient beings that are part of our national soul.

But the wild horse was also at the very heart of a range war with his demise as the ultimate goal. It all had to do with control of public lands across the western states. In the Wild Horse And Burro Act of 1971, the BLM and the National Forest Service were appointed to administer 52 million acres of Federal land that were designated by that law to be *devoted principally to the welfare of wild horses and burros* in *a thriving natural ecological balance.* According to Craig

Downer, Ph.D. in Wildlife Ecology, these two government agencies disregarded the law and reduced that 52 million acres by approximately 36% and then leased more than 95% of that which remained to cattle and sheep ranchers.

Making matters worse, these ranchers convinced the government to allow them to hunt and eliminate the cougar, bear, and the wolf because these three predators were killing and eating their cattle and sheep. The cougar, bear and the wolf, like the wild horse, are historically indigenous species that are supposed to be living under the protection of the government on federal lands. They are also the natural predators of the wild horse, so without these predators in place, the herds multiply faster than they would otherwise. Multiply faster into a world where their forage and water is being consumed by cattle and sheep that effectively outnumber them by more than 150 to one. On land that by law is to be *devoted principally to the welfare of wild horses and burros* in *a thriving natural ecological balance.*

So rather than enforcing the terms of the law by removing the cattle and sheep which would allow the horses and burros to once again be the *principle presence* on the land and allow the *natural ecological balance* to return wherein the cougar, bear, and wolf would flourish, the BLM has stated to the media that the land will not support the number of wild horses and burros living on it so their numbers must be reduced. At this writing more than 33,000 mustangs have been captured and put in holding pens around the country. Not because the land will not support 60,000 horses but because it will not support that many horses plus at least a million for-profit cattle and sheep.

Kathleen and I were in a fog of déjà vu. Like when we discovered how the horse was really supposed to live. We had to be nuts. If all this were true wouldn't people know about it? Wouldn't they act on the knowledge? Surely we were missing something.

There's more.

The ranchers were not satisfied with being able to lease the land and water rights for well under the market value of comparable privately held land. Nor were they satisfied with being able to hunt the natural predators of the horse. They wanted the wild horses off the land entirely. Many of these ranchers were actively campaigning to get the 1971 law repealed by trying to convince the government, the media, and the lay public that the horses don't belong on these lands because they are not native. Not indigenous. The federal government is only obligated to protect *native* wildlife. Their claim was that the mustang is merely feral. Domesticated horses that had escaped from the Spanish, the Indians, and the cavalry. Feral like the cats who leave home to live in the back alleys of New York.

Their claim simply ignores the historic and scientific truth in pursuit of financial gain.

The wild horse is as native and indigenous to North America as the Bengal tiger is to India or the lion is to Africa. The wild horse was born here in the region that was to become Idaho, Utah and Wyoming and fully evolved over a period of 52 million years. Between 7600 and 10,000 years ago an unknown cataclysm apparently wiped out the horse in North America along with numerous other species including the saber-toothed tiger. But not before the horse had migrated across the Bering Strait Land Bridge and spread into the rest of the world. Then in the early sixteenth century the horse was re-introduced to his homeland by the Spanish Conquistadores.

He became what is termed reintroduced native wildlife.

If for some reason a plague wiped out the tiger in India and the species was re-introduced from, say, wild animal park inventory that had originally come from India would those tigers be considered native, indigenous?

Or feral?

Absolutely the former.

Remains of the earliest animal anywhere in the world to bear recognizably horse-like anatomy were found in the Idaho-Utah-Wyoming area dating 52 million years ago. For the serious student the entire chronology from that point to the fully evolved horse in North America is detailed in the Resources section at the back of this book.

And there is no doubt that when the Spanish brought the horse to America they were bringing him home. Back to his native land. Wearing the same genetics, the same DNA sequencing he was wearing when he left and when those left behind were wiped out.

Some wildlife groups consider the bighorn sheep and the American bison "native" to North America. However, both species actually evolved in Asia and came into North America via the Bering Strait Land Bridge. The horse, *Equus caballus*, conversely, evolved exclusively in North America and crossed the Bering Strait bridge into Siberia, traveling in the other direction.

So conversation that leads anyone to believe that the wild horse is anything other than "reintroduced native wild-life" is folly. Or worse yet malevolent.

As I write this the 33,000 wild mustangs residing in government holding pens and facilities around the country amount to more than half of all the remaining wild mustangs in existence.

And those remaining in the wild are living below viable levels. Which simply put means below the number that must be available for breeding to keep the horse from not being forced into incest for the species to attempt to survive.

All because of those cattle and sheep. *Illegal* cattle and sheep. To allow all this to happen the 1971 law had to knowingly be broken.

I was astounded. And embarrassed that I didn't know any of this before.

And sad.

Made sadder when I learned that the Government Accountability Office was recommending death for the 33,000 wild mustangs in government custody because it was costing too much to feed and care for them.

The OED definition of *domestication* scratched and clawed its way back into my consciousness.

To civilize.

OED's assumption of course was that humans would be doing the *civilizing*.

Perhaps humans are the ones *needing* it.

5

A NEW LAND

The golden stallion shook off the chill of night air and wandered through the herd checking for injuries after the long run. As usual there were none. Not even among the young. He paused to watch two foals frolicking and tussling with each other, each barely a month old. Unlike many stallions he felt that a new foal was noble and he would always treat it so. Perhaps the quality of his lineage and all that his ancestors had been through had somehow found its way into genetic code. Or maybe it had always been there.

The stallion had never known a home other than this rocky arid high desert. But the blood of another who had traveled the entire breadth of this great land ran through his veins. And that of one who had saved his herd from shipwreck. The stallion had once again passed on this splendid heritage. But the world around these new youngsters was changing, and not for the better.

The lush grasses were gone, water was scarce, and there was severe competition for what little remained. The grass had once stretched forever. Men were few and those few understood the horse, some seeming not unlike a horse themselves. They would come and sit and wait. With kind and caring eyes. Off at a distance. Alone. Just watching. Eventually the curiosity of one horse or another would stir a relationship, which would soon become a bond, and man and horse would leave together. As it was with one of the stallion's favorite colts, but the stallion didn't seem to mind. The young colt wasn't forced. It was his choice to go. And he would soon need to be banished from the herd anyway. There can only be one stallion.

The humans the stallion had encountered recently were different. Their eyes were not kind, nor their actions. And they came with thundering machines.

The big palomino turned away from the setting sun and lifted his head toward the sky sniffing the evening breeze. The smell was sweet, like rain and fresh ripe grass. Like times past. He wondered how far the wind had come.

The buckskin had her nose in the air as well, acknowledging the new scent. She glanced at the stallion and their eyes locked for a moment, their minds intertwined. She had joined the herd only three years before when she was discovered alone except for a younger filly and very nervous in a small canyon with a stream. She wore the scars of a life longer than her years.

The mare returned to her job scanning the horizon. It's the same whenever any horse lies down. The herd gathers and guards. The sentinel watches and listens. Every horse needs REM sleep but cannot get it standing up. Lying on the ground they are more vulnerable to predators so most horses will not lie down unless a guard is in place. One of the reasons why nature never intended horses to live in isolation.

The stallion watched the mare for a moment, then turned and once again gazed off in the direction of the wind.

6

FIRST TOUCH

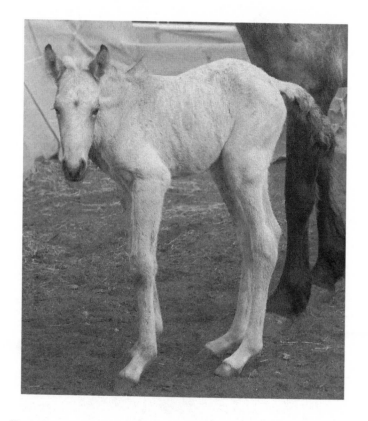

I had never laid hands on an unhandled horse.

    Or touched a new foal, handled or otherwise.

    Never mind one conceived in the wild.

    So you might think I'd be nervous.

For reasons unknown I didn't think I was. I was just anxious. Excited. At least that's what I kept telling myself.

The appropriate term, I believe, is *naïve*.

Very, very naïve.

I was able to separate Malachi from his unhandled mom on the second day of his life. He was all legs and already using them. Running, jumping, kicking. And I so looked forward to that first touch. He was, after all, so-o-o cute.

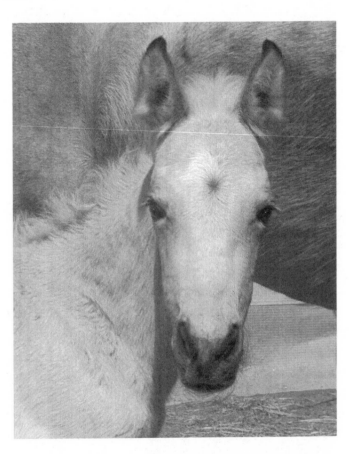

But when I approached him and touched him for the first time my adrenaline shot up like a geyser and my heart seemed to erupt.

What is this? I scolded myself.

Kathleen and I were newcomers to the horse world but we had worked and studied hard during our short three years and one thing I knew: horses read your adrenaline like a book and theirs will match yours every time. Calm is good.

But quite suddenly I wasn't calm. I had learned to squash adrenaline whenever it was necessary with our herd on the hill. But on this day and with this baby the switches and levers were not working. I had no control. I debated calling off the session. Would I be wasting my time if I couldn't convince this brand new horse that I was a calm - thus trustworthy - pal to hang out with?

I backed away for a bit, taking long slow breaths. Hoping my adrenaline would retreat.

It didn't.

Slowly, painfully, I began to realize what this was all about.

What if I wasn't up to the task?

This was a mustang. Conceived in the wild. I had so much planned for him, including this book. A brand new journey. A new way of looking at horses. All horses. And quite suddenly here he was. And I was just standing there.

Could I really do this? Did I have the stuff?

An editorial in the New York Times following the euthanasia of the race horse Barbaro spoke of horses in these words: *You would have to look a long, long time to find a dishonest or cruel horse. And the odds are that if you did find one, it*

was made cruel or dishonest by the company it kept with humans.
It is no exaggeration to say that nearly every horse is pure of
heart.

I believed that.

Finally.

And I wanted to prove it to everyone.

But was I up to the task?

The mustang protection program in this country was in a shambles and this little boy was to be an icon of everything it should and could be. The emotional link between the taxpayers and how their money was really being spent.

But I had to do it alone. Just me and our new boy horse. It had to be personal. To both of us. Otherwise the emotional link wouldn't read true. I had to be invested, out on the end of the diving board. Leaping off into the deep water.

I spent time every day with our other horses. Mixing with them in the herd. Loving them. Leading them. Being one of them. Little Malachi was genetically programmed exactly like the rest of the herd, like every other horse on the planet.

So why was I so freaked out?

I couldn't answer the question. I had read the books, watched the videos, talked to experts who raised multiple foals every year. But I had never actually touched one. Felt one move and wriggle under my hands. I had no idea how strong he was. Or how he would take to me. And I had forgotten how much we depend upon the nuances that come only with experience until they aren't there for us to call on.

Apparently all of this scared me to death.

He's two days old, I kept telling myself. Get a grip.

He was pacing nervously wanting to get back to his mom and she was having a hissy fit, huffing, puffing, and snorting. I so wanted to just open the gate and let him return.

But I didn't. I walked over and wrapped my arms around him and rubbed him all over. But even as I held him and rubbed him I could feel myself trembling.

I scanned down the mental checklist. A finger in his mouth. Rub his tongue. Play with his ears, inside and out. Lift his feet. And still my heart wouldn't stop racing. It helped when he stepped on me the first time and I found that it didn't hurt. And when he tried to get away once and I realized that I was actually stronger than he was. That wouldn't last long I kept telling myself. *So you must do this right, and do it now.*

I struggled through the drill but I was a mess. I had no idea how much of a mess until I played back the video Kathleen was shooting during the session. She kept the camera rolling, playing reporter, after Malachi was back in the paddock with his mom.

"So how was your first session ever with a new foal? How'd it go?"

I didn't expect the question and just stared at her blank-faced for an incredibly long time. When I finally said something I sounded like I was about to fall completely apart. My voice was quivering. I was shaking. And trying much too hard to sound like I had a clue when I really didn't.

Yet later that night I couldn't shut up about it. I had actually touched that boy. And gotten him to relax, and even to follow me at one point of his own choice.

"Did I tell you about when he followed me?"

"I was there dear," Kathleen said. "I saw it. And yes, you told me. Three times now."

"I touched his umbilical cord by accident and it scared me."

" I think all of it scared you. But you did it. You *did* do it."

"I did, didn't I?"

We just sat for the longest time, each of us replaying the moments.

I was smitten. Consumed.

In the afterglow of the session, I knew I could do this. The nerves would be out there on edge for a while, until those nuances of experience began to kick in. But I was certain I could do it. *We* could do it. Malachi and me. Which is the way I had prescribed it must be. Just the two of us, each making our own mistakes and trying to work through them.

Trial and error life. I had no experience but the experts all had to start somewhere. This boy could teach me as I was teaching him. We could learn about each other together. I was criticized for this. If I made a mistake or did the wrong thing I could ruin this foal, or so I was told. I could alienate his mom. I should leave it to the experts.

But I simply couldn't.

I was afraid. But those first touches brought this old soul to life in a way that I will never forget, and probably will never be able to fully explain.

This was my boy. I was the first human to ever touch him. How could I ask him to trust me if I couldn't even trust myself?

I had to figure it out.

For Malachi.

And for me.

And hopefully for you.

But I'm getting ahead of myself.

7

NOELLE

How did I get here?

What was I doing lying on the ground, on my stomach, completely ignoring the wild mustang not thirty feet away. Or trying to.

Insanity, I thought. I'm sixty-nine years old for God's sake.

Would famous horse trainer Monty Roberts do this? Or Pat Parelli? Or Clinton Anderson? All those guys whose DVDs I had consumed so diligently when horses first came into our lives. Would any of these men be lying down belly first in a paddock just inches away from an untouched wild mustang?

I don't think so.

And yet there I was. And there was this mustang. This *wild* mustang.

Is that *wild* like in *wild* tiger? Or *wild* cougar?

A very short time ago that question wouldn't have come up. At that point I still had my faculties.

I've been known to say that life is not a spectator sport. Life is to *live*, not to watch. Life is to experience. And there

I was, lying on the ground, staring off this mustang, apparently practicing what I preach.

Did I say *wild* mustang?

Kathleen drove by and for a moment she thought I was dead.

He died in the pasture with his new adopted mustang. It was his Christmas present from me. I should've known better. Did the mustang kill him? Stomp him to death? What happened? Wait, he moved. He's not dead. He's just crazy.

Certifiable.

But with passion.

A mere three years before we hadn't yet acquired our first horse. Sprinting from that moment to owning seven horses and outlining a book took less than a year. Don't ask what I was thinking.

It was an obsessive period, running seemingly at light speed, learning about horses, living with them, researching, making mistakes, re-learning, and ultimately discovering that something was very wrong in this world of horses.

We were always racing forward to the next problem, the next plateau, laying out the book, writing, finding an agent, finding a publisher, promoting, making more mistakes and still learning more about horses. We never really slowed down enough to look back at what had been accomplished. To fully realize, to absorb, to enjoy.

And we had no idea where it was all leading. *Just tell us please how one is supposed to properly take care of a horse. Or seven.* What did they need? How were they supposed to live? How should we approach them? I suppose the pivotal point was the day my Cash arrived. I had discovered the wild horse studies of Monty Roberts. How and why horses communicate, socialize, and trust each other. So I took Cash immediately into the round pen and, using Monty's techniques and language, gave Cash the choice of whether or not he wanted to be in relationship with me. Many owners and trainers deny the horse that choice, forcing him into submission. But Monty's concepts are based upon letting the horse make the decision, on his own. And when he does, everything changes.

It was a scary moment because rejection is not one of my favorite concepts. What would I to do if Cash said *no thanks?* Mercifully the question didn't come up. And when he walked up behind me and touched me on the shoulder saying *I trust you to be my leader* it did, in fact, change everything. Cash has never stopped trying, never stopped giving. And I was no longer a horse owner. I was a friend, a companion, a partner, a leader. And I vowed at that moment I would do the very best for him that I possibly could.

The problem was: we didn't really know what that was. We didn't know how to evaluate *the very best.* That's when I began asking questions. A *lot* of questions. And slowly we began to realize that many of the answers we were getting simply didn't make any sense. It wasn't long before Kathleen and I began to feel that we must be missing something because the manner in which most horses were being kept and cared for seemed very wrong when evaluated against the answers we were now finding.

We kept digging, searching for that missing piece, for how could we, who had no experience whatsoever, be discovering things that folks with decades of experience didn't know? It seemed like a silly notion. But as the puzzle pieces began to come together something else began to stir, like a baby chick pecking and poking its way out of an egg. I found myself toying with the idea of writing about this bizarre, funny, sad, amazing, and incredibly enlightening journey.

Kathleen said the title of the book should've been *Google It,* because that's where I spent every waking moment when I wasn't out with the horses. Devouring studies, scientific papers, and archives. Which eventually lead me into the middle of a herd of wild horses living free out in the American west. It was there that the traditional thinking about horses cracked and crumbled. I discovered that equine genetics had been designed and developed over roughly fifty-two million years to help a prey animal survive in the wild. A prey animal who had no defenses whatsoever against predators except to flee. Genetics that were designed to live in wide open spaces where predators can be seen from long distances. Genetics that require living in a herd because there is safety in numbers. And require moving eight to twenty miles a day, all while eating small bits of mostly grass for eighteen to twenty hours a day to suit the tiny tummy and digestive system of this unique species.

Quite simply all of this blew me away. I suppose I had probably thought that horses were born with metal shoes nailed to their feet. I had no idea that horses, genetically, are wide open space dwellers and that to confine them causes nothing but stress which over time manifests itself in all sorts of negative ways including illness and reduction of life span. Dogs like small cozy rooms. People like small cozy rooms.

So why wouldn't horses? Because dogs and humans are predatory cave dwellers. Horses are not. Confinement equals stress.

Our heads were swimming.

We discovered that every horse on the planet, whether wild or domestic, would prefer to be in relationship. Yes, even with predators, if they could be.

Why?

Because the horse's number one concern in life is safety and security. That singular concern drives all of the behavior that so many humans define as negative, undisciplined, or even mean when, in reality, it is behavior induced by hard-wired fear.

A trusting relationship with a predator would result in one less major concern for the horse. One less worry. The odds of that happening with a tiger or a cougar are slim and none. Those predators must attempt to eat the horse to stay alive. But the odds that it can happen with most humans are very good. *If* we choose to approach the relationship on a basis of trust, not dominance; *if* we give the horse the choice of whether he wants to be in relationship with us or not – in other words making it *his* decision, not ours - and *if* we take the time to understand - *really* understand - how to communicate our wishes to the horse in a non-dominant non-violent way and in a manner that he can truly comprehend.

Which usually takes a boatload of persistence and patience.

One of those two I'm not even remotely familiar with. Patience.

Some would say I've never even heard of the word. Or *hadn't* until I met up with horses.

They are still teaching me with every encounter.

And that's where this story begins.

And why I was lying on the ground that day, on my belly, in a large paddock, with an unrestrained wild mustang who had never touched or willingly been touched by a human in her entire seven-plus years of life. Or so said the BLM, but looking back I believe they had under-estimated her age. There were no records relating to her birth, no records at all actually. This is important, I discovered later, because no one in the know wants to adopt an old mustang. It seems the longer they are in the wild – in other words the longer they stay alive in the wild – the stronger is their fear quotient, because that's what keeps them alive. I've since been told that the best age to adopt is at one to two years old. Three at the most. And this was an older wild mustang whose experience with humans so far had been totally negative. Not physically abusive so far as we know, but definitely emotionally abusive. She had been ripped away from her home, away from her family band, away from the only lifestyle she had ever known and plopped down in a Bureau of Land Management (BLM) holding pen, then into a paddock with this human predator who was acting very strangely. He was lying flat on the ground.

I wanted to separate myself from any prior human experience she might've had.

I wanted to say to her as quickly and emphatically as possible that I totally trusted her. *I am not here to hurt you or to eat you.*

So I had placed myself in the most vulnerable position I could think of.

I wouldn't do this with just any horse. But I had looked into this mustang's eyes and found kindness in her spirit. I trusted her and I wanted her to know it. So, hopefully, she would begin a journey of trust with me. What I couldn't see in those eyes is how much fear was locked up inside. Fear so firmly burned into her soul that there was little if anything she could do about it. I've seen it so often with her over the years. Seen her want so desperately to do something I was encouraging but she was physically unable to cross the threshold. Just couldn't do it.

Looking back I realize there was a huge lesson in play here. A living verification, a proof if you will, that horses are not mean-spirited, aggressive, or unwilling by nature unless they have been made so by their human associations. But their fear is often read as stubborn, recalcitrant behavior. So the horse is punished, which generates more fear. And so it goes.

All horses are prey animals, flight animals. The fear reaction is instinctive, involuntary, genetic. *React first and ask questions later.* It's hard-wired. With a mustang, especially an older one who has lived in the wild for six or seven or eight years it's exponentially worse because that hard-wired reactive nature is cultivated every day, many times a day from the moment the horse is born. A domesticated horse raised in a loving compassionate, understanding environment will soon learn that he or she is living in a relatively safe place and that everything that moves is not necessarily a predator. A foal, even a mustang foal, who is imprinted by a caring, compassionate human immediately after birth avoids many of the things that later can generate fear once the genetics have kicked in. But a prey animal living in the wild must react to everything that moves. From the moment the horse is born she is taught to put that genetic fear onto high alert. Noelle could be a poster horse for this way of life. But she has never once shown me the first hint of aggressive behavior. It's not in her bones.

Noelle has been with us almost four years as I write this and she has yet to have a single hoof trimmed or accept a halter or lead rope. Only recently has she trusted me enough to let me safely cut off the halter that was placed on her when we picked her up at the BLM facility in Reno. Saffron, our second pregnant mustang, is the polar opposite. She was standing calmly getting her feet trimmed mere months after coming to us from the BLM. She accepts a halter, and leads to a loose line. Which isn't really necessary because she comes to a call and walks with me wherever I ask. These are two very different mustangs. Probably with different backgrounds in the wild. Possibly different encounters with Bureau of Land Management personnel. And, unfortunately, very different encounters with me.

I learned that the tiniest mistake with a mustang, especially an older mustang, made before the bond has been established, at her choice, amplifies the fear quotient exponentially. I clipped a lead line onto her BLM halter way, way too early and it scared her to death. She ran for at least ten minutes with this long lead rope chasing her like a snake. She has yet to erase it completely from her memory banks.

But she taught us a huge lesson. More than one actually. She taught us to never ever do anything whatsoever that could possibly under any circumstances evoke a fear response in a mustang, or any horse who has yet to say *I trust you*. And she taught us all about No Agenda Time. We just didn't realize it at the moment.

Had I introduced her to No Agenda Time (see Resources) right at the beginning and made no moves to attempt *any*thing with her that could even possibly evoke fear until well after she had, of her own free will, committed to trust us, I believe things would've been very different. But without the experience with her exactly as it happened, I never would've known any of that. And without Noelle, Saffron would never have experienced No Agenda Time. Nor would she be where she is today.

Noelle will be there someday. Now it's just a matter of time.

One morning when I walked into the paddock where Saffy and Stormy were spending their nights before they joined the herd in the pasture, Saffy meandered toward me as she always does for her good morning rub and greeting. But she pulled up short when I was maybe six feet away and as I continued to approach she turned away with a huff and a puff, a signal I've grown very used to from Noelle. A signal indicating *Oh my. There's something new here! Something scary. Time to react first and ask questions later.* Then I remembered I had a small Tupperware container in one hand (to fill with diatomaceous earth and take back to the house). I paused, talked to her a bit, held out the container and said *Have a sniff. C'mon Saffy, have a sniff.* She learned the term during our evening No Agenda Time.

On this morning she just stood for the longest, not looking away but not giving the container (or me) two eyes either. For maybe ten seconds. Then she turned and looked it right in the tupper. It didn't bite her so, after a moment, she reached and sniffed the container, let out a breath, and it was over. I gave her a morning rub on the face, rubbed the container down her forehead, and proceeded to the tack room. Done.

Later that same morning, I was feeding Noelle in the round pen. The pocket of my treat/tool/med vest was bulging, unusually so, with several items I had just crammed into it, and it was therefore... *different!* This different pocket, which was always there, *every* morning and every evening, just not bulging so, touched Noelle as I was reaching across her neck to scratch her off-side.

WHOA!

Gone.

That fast. A full roll-back leaving her a good eight feet away from me. I reached down and held the horse-eating bulging pocket out to her, talking softly, asking her to have a sniff. But the closer the pocket got the father away she moved. She would have none of it. Zero.

Ultimately she came back but she would not sniff the pocket. Every time I asked she would pull away again. *No way. Not happening.* And therein lies the chasm of difference between Miss Saffron and Miss Noelle.

I'm certain that part of this is their age difference. Added to the fact that we were four years further down the "road of experience" when we adopted Saffy. Overlaid by the mistakes with and lessons from Noelle.

Before Saffron came we had already decided to do absolutely nothing with her until, by her own choice, she had accepted us. Until she told us very clearly that she trusted us. We began No Agenda Time on her second evening here and still continue it today. More for us now than for her. It took Saffron only 35 days to make a decision.

But still, these are two vastly different wild horses. Saffy is much younger. According to the BLM she was barely three when her baby was conceived in the wild. And still three when she was rounded up. Perhaps still three when we adopted her. Or barely four. Our vet agrees. The BLM said that Noelle was a late six when she was rounded up, probably seven when we adopted her. Possibly older. And these are very critical years between her and Saffy.

Critical, because at three to four a horse is still a child. Her growth plates do not even complete their fusing until late five-to-six years old. And our experience with Miss Mouse (an American Saddlebred rescued at less than a year old) was that she did not begin to develop her adult-like maturity until she was approaching six years old. Until then she was very full of herself, always playing and cavorting like a baby (*See the Video of Mouse at Three on The Soul of a Horse You Tube Channel, and on Vimeo*).

What this told us is that a mustang at three or four in the wild probably hasn't yet matured enough to seriously take full responsibility for her own safety. She is taught from birth to respond to her genetic fear quotient *React first and ask questions later*. That little edge in time keeps the horse alive if a wolf or a cougar shows up. But until adulthood, if Mouse is any example, horses are more prone to react to other horses' reaction to fear than to their own. In other words, they are trusting – at least to some degree – their herd members to be their primary fear trigger rather than taking responsibility for it themselves. As she approached six Miss Mouse became noticeably more reactive to first-hand stimuli. Until that change her freaky leaps in adrenaline were almost always either 1) in reaction to other horses reacting to something or 2) waking up out in the pasture and suddenly realizing that she was all alone. Her herd mates had wandered off. *Yikes!!!* And off she'd race to find them! Today, not so much. If she realizes she's alone she'll either say *so what*, or just wander back to wherever the herd is and settle in, secure in her own ability and awareness.

So... in other words. A three-to-four year old mustang (or younger) is likely going to be much more willing to trust some other horse – or a human who proves worthy – because she probably doesn't yet fully trust herself (Saffron). A 6-7-8 year old who has fully learned to trust and rely on her own instincts and warnings has had the experience to see first hand how well her instincts work when she reacts first and asks questions later (Noelle). Which, again, is probably why we keep hearing around the horse world: if you're going to adopt a mustang, adopt a young one.

Does that mean I would trade Noelle? Of course not. I love her dearly. And deep down I know she at least tries to love me. And wants to do more than her highly sharpened instinct will allow her to do. You can see it in her eyes. And her actions.

What I didn't know then but now believe is that every fear of human is caused by human. The current human, or some past human. Somewhere. At some time. And therefore can be associated with all humans. See Chapter 29.

But, for now I will just be Noelle's friend and allow her the time her instincts require. I completely refuse to cowboy her in any way.

And I thank God from the depths of my heart for showing me that I needed to know both Noelle and Mouse before I could really know Saffron.

So there we were. This mustang and me. Noelle was completely unrestrained. I didn't have the assistance or safety of a small stall, or even a control rope. She was free to do whatever her heart told her to do. And at the very least she was being curious because, in a way, I was speaking her language. I was offering her vulnerability which is how horses communicate trust to each other.

She had only arrived the night before after a twelve-hour trailer ride from the BLM facility in Reno. The day was December 20th.

I spent time with her every day thereafter. Nineteen days passed before she would take her favorite feed from a bowl in my hand. On Day 25 I touched her for the first time, a rub on her cheek. Every day I continued to see in her eyes that she wanted more than she could give, at least at that moment. When no food was offered, if I reached out slowly to touch her cheek, she would turn, even slower, just an inch or two... as if to say: I must turn away. I don't want to really so I'll just move slower than you so your hand will catch up. But I don't catch up. I stop where her head was, and smile, and withdraw.

One of the amazements to me was that she wanted so much, and seemed so calm and trusting, but that didn't really translate into crossing thresholds. Several times she went to sleep just inches from my chest and I had to seriously concentrate on issuing no vibes, no movements, or even thoughts... which had its own issues because when I was concentrating so hard on not disrupting her trust I knew there was anxiety creeping through my every pore.

By Day 60 I could rub her right side with my left hand, but not my right hand. And her left side with my right hand, but not the left. And on occasions I could clean out the corners of her eyes. With the appropriate hand. And on Day 60 the vet pointed out that she was bagging up.

"Meaning?" I asked.

"Getting close to having a baby."

"But you said May!" I exclaimed. The date was February 18 and we were not ready! Not even close.

Malachi was born on March 3rd.

8

THE INTRUDERS

The herd had come a long way. Following the wind, urged on by the scent of fine grasses and fresh clean water. They were well beyond their home range, their usual grazing area. This made the stallion and the matriarch uneasy but they forged ahead, the matriarch leading with the buckskin at her side and the stallion pushing from behind, all certain of their reward.

Horses in the wild are nomadic, often moving as many as thirty miles in a single twenty-four hour day, but usually within a loosely defined area that never puts known grazing and water sources out of reach. A herd might consist of hundreds of horses but is almost always an assembly of smaller bands made up of five to twelve mares, their offspring, and a single stallion. At times the bands of a herd will gather together for protection but once the threat has passed they will disperse back into these smaller bands. Sometimes the bands will travel together. Other times not. But for a single band to be so far from their home range and the rest of the herd was unusual indeed.

The matriarch was tiring and the stallion knew he was stretching the limits of their safety, and their safety was his job. He sniffed the air but the breeze had vanished and there was no scent. Perhaps they should stop for a rest.

The notion apparently reached the matriarch for she and the buckskin paused on the edge of a craggy slope. The stallion joined them and there, spreading out down the slope below them, was their destination. A valley with a crystal clear stream running through gently rolling hills covered in green grasses. The stallion uttered a soft nicker. A pleased nicker. His band was going to eat well for a change. His instincts had been right. The mares and youngsters waited as the stallion evaluated the small valley. Both ends were open and it was actually accessible down the slope so there was little chance of being trapped by a predator. He and the matriarch exchanged a look and she turned and began to make her way down the hill. The others followed.

It was a peaceful little valley. And quiet. The first to sprawl out on the grass for a sleep were the youngest foals. They had nursed and kicked up their heels and now the long trek was taking its toll. But it was a short nap. The stallion heard it first and spun toward the sound of hundreds, maybe thousands, of cows tromping into the valley. Normally that wouldn't be of concern. Horses live in concert with other grazers. Deer, antelope, even cattle. But there were so many and they were all moving as if in a hurry. Something about it didn't feel right. Then the big palomino saw men. Driving the cattle. On horses.

He wheeled and screamed a warning. Instantly the herd was on the move following the matriarch up the same slope they had traversed down earlier. At the top the stallion turned and gazed down on the valley. It was filled with cows.

Consumed by cows. The stallion had never seen so many cows. And there were more still coming. His small band of horses had come so far to find good forage. And good water. He tossed his head toward the sky and bellowed in anguish.

Then he turned and followed the herd away.

Below, one of the men on horseback watched the big stallion retreat. He retrieved a small black object from his jacket, jabbed it a couple of times with a finger and held it to his ear.

9

UNTIL SAFFRON

Four years passed. A lot happened.

And a lot didn't.

On the evening of Malachi's three-month birthday, June 3rd, a rogue storm passed through our area and frightened him. He woke up running, searching for his mama, not watching where he was going. He smashed headfirst into a post, snapped his brain stem, and died instantly.

We were devastated. Our hearts were breaking. They still are.

He was our first and then only baby horse. We only wanted one. And so much of the rest of my life was wrapped up in him. I so looked forward to going down at feeding times because Malachi got to come out with me at liberty and play while I loaded the gator for the pasture feed.

He was such a good boy. And so big, and strong, and healthy. Everything you could ask for in a messenger for the mustangs; and he represented everything we had learned in *The Soul of a Horse*, our entire journey. His birth was to be the first chapter of my next book. I loved him so, and so looked forward to the rest of my life with my boy horse. It was all so random. So wrong. I couldn't stop crying, and as I recap this I'm at it again.

He almost single-handedly changed out vet's mind about all the non-traditional things we were doing. Dr. Matt is the vet for a 140-horse breeding farm across town. He saw babies virtually every day of his life but said he had never seen a baby like Malachi.

He was fascinated by him and would come by and just stand at the fence and watch Malachi romp around the steep rocky paddock. I think he loved him as much as we did. This baby horse who broke all the rules. He was born under the stars with nobody watching but God and his mama.

The foaling book told us that after a couple of weeks he could come outside for two hours a day. We laughed, because Malachi had never been *inside*. He was running up and down the hill and around rocks and boulders on his third or fourth day of life and I remember Kathleen saying, "Just think of all the babies who never get a chance to do this."

Because Noelle had never had a lead rope on and was very possessive and protective we had to figure out how to separate them so I could begin the imprinting process. He was in my lap on his fourth day. He wore his first halter on Day 9 and by Day 11 was leading in every direction on a loose line. By Day 13 he was stepping up onto his platform.

On that day he even went up once by himself when my back was turned. I looked back and I swear he was actually beaming with pride. I couldn't keep myself from laughing out loud. I wrote this line on our blog: "How does life get better than this :) Now if I could just get this strapping young boy to pass the good word on to his mom."

But he didn't get the chance. He would return to us in a few years and in his own way be responsible for Saffron coming into our family. But for now, God had other things for him to do. Before he left us, Malachi was proving every day that deep down every horse on the planet would prefer to be in relationship than not.

Prefer.

But not always able.

Noelle continued to try really hard. To want to respond. But her fear response was still at high alert. One day, after we moved to Tennessee, while she was eating in the round pen, I walked over to check one of the panels. On the way back to my traditional rubbing post next to her, I stepped on the plastic tarp wadded up in the middle of the pen and Noelle spun and leaped to the far side of the pen.

"Noelle, Noelle," I chided softly. "You've been eating along side this tarp forever. Now, come on back over here."

I held out my hand, palm down, fingers slightly curled.

"Come on. Come give me a hug."

Not a real hug. I hold out my hand, and she presses it with her face or forehead. We call it a hug.

She walked over and gave me a hug, then resumed eating her dinner as I rubbed her neck, and back, and belly.

All as if nothing whatsoever had happened.

Just this morning when Noelle went into the round pen for breakfast, Mariah followed her in, an eye on Noelle's bucket in my hand. I had to raise my voice to move her out. Which sent Noelle's adrenaline soaring and she wanted to leave as well. She wouldn't even take the treat she usually takes before I fill her tub. Normally she comes into the round pen on her own and I always hold out her treat.

"Good girl Miss Noelle. Here's your tweety."

Yes, that's what we call it. I think we're both adults, but maybe not.

Some days she'll walk right up to me and take the treat from my hand as if it were the most normal thing to do in the world. Without a blink. Other days she'll stop a few feet short and reach way out, even her lips reaching, then pull back without taking the treat. Then maybe she'll try one more time but just can't bring herself to go for it. Finally she'll duck her head under my hand and push up on my fingers, saying as clearly as if she were using words: *I just can't do it today. I just can't. May I just go ahead and have my dinner?*

She's been out with our herd for almost four years, and has been the herd leader. The dominant. But in the small confinement of the barn breezeway, or the round pen, she can be totally intimidated by even the lowest horse on the herd totem pole. Mouse learned some time ago that if she came charging into the round pen, running straight for No-elle, Noelle would freak out and race away leaving her feed bowl for Mouse to consume.

In the pasture that kind of bluff won't work. Noelle merely spins threatening to boot Mouse into next week and Mouse quickly retreats. I mean *quickly*.

But in the round pen, even if there are three gates open, something about the tight quarters and fast movement does her in. Like the sound of me stepping on a tarp.

She obviously doesn't fully trust any horse or human, including me. Or if she does it's not enough to belay her hard-wired fear response. She wants to. She usually comes back quickly. But anything sudden or out of the ordinary still brings extreme reaction. She simply cannot help herself. One day I can be rubbing all over her, combing her mane, scratching her feet. And some days, although rare, I might not even be able to touch her.

I suppose I had come to believe that this is just the way mustangs are. Or I simply wasn't up to the task. Or both. I was reconciled to just being her friend while chipping away at her fears the tiniest amount at a time.

Until Saffron.

It took us three years after Malachi died to even consider another pregnant mustang. And only then because one popped up nearby that had recently been adopted from the BLM on a very special date.

The date of adoption was March 3rd.

Malachi's birthday.

He was still communicating.

We figured that God had a hand in this so there was no way to not check into it.

And indeed God did have a hand in it, but as it turned out that horse showed up just to get our attention. To rekindle the fires. She already had a happy home. But like so often is the case, God was going to have to slap me around a bit to get me to listen. To figure it out.

The clue came when we learned that the pregnant mustang in question had been adopted from the BLM's facility on the campus of the Piney Woods School just south of Jackson, Mississippi.

The same Piney Woods School where I have been a member of the board of trustees for almost 25 years.

I knew the BLM had leased land from the school but my impression of their facility was one designed to gentle a few mustangs at a time to make them more adoptable. But it turns out it was merely a holding facility like the one in Reno where we had adopted Noelle.

How convenient.

And it just so happened they had one pregnant mustang for adoption.

A palomino.

Oh my.

If you can't guess, you'll come to know why that got our attention.

We were sent photos. She was due in May. This was March 14, a Wednesday. We wanted to schedule a visit to see her and confirm but the BLM was holding an open adoption event for the public on the coming weekend and their policy was strictly first come first adopt.

Even Kathleen, a supreme advocate of *no more horses*, said, "I guess we have no choice. Adopt her now and we'll drive down Friday night and pick her up Saturday morning. She looks sweet."

She didn't know at the time how important that decision was. Yet another God thing.

With one phone call our herd leaped a third in size.

On Saturday morning she did nothing at all to worry us during our pasture viewings. But when they drove a group from that pasture into the pens so they could sort her out for loading she started kicking every horse in sight.

"Oh no," from Kathleen. "She looked so sweet."

When she was in the chute to have her ID tag removed we made eye contact and there was something special going on in that pretty head. I eased my hand onto one of the rails of the chute panel and she turned, thought for a moment about it, and reached out for a sniff. Kathleen was on the video camera and felt it coming. She dropped the still camera and slowly zoomed the video camera in to meet this young lady's flexing nostril on my fingers (See the video *Here We Go Again* on The Soul of a Horse You Tube Channel). I could feel the warmth of her breath. A shiver skittered up my back.

"Are you pretty certain about her delivery date in May?" I asked the BLM facility manager.

"Well…" he drew this out slowly. "I think it's going to be a bit sooner. I just noticed she's bagging up."

Back when we adopted Noelle our vet had told us that a mare should not travel during the last 30 days of pregnancy.

I asked the facility manager about that and he said he felt we were fine. It wasn't that far from Piney Woods back to middle Tennessee and he was pretty certain she had just begun to bag up.

Did he want to encourage the adoption?

I'm sure he did.

Did we want to get her home?

No question.

So we were in agreement.

The gate was opened and Saffron trotted without complaint into our trailer. And off we went.

It was the right decision.

Three days later baby Firestorm was born.

10

FOREVER CHANGED

The filly was coming of age. Gone were the romps around the herd with other youngsters. The playing, pawing, and nipping, then racing off to hide behind her mother. Only yesterday she was a foal, a baby. And now she was old enough to have a baby of her own. She had grown up big and strong, and like her mama, was a beautifully dappled buckskin. Her father, the band stallion, was solid black without marking. A very handsome daddy, and very smart. The filly adored him and was frantic that he was not with them.

Twice the machine in the air had come and frightened them and twice the stallion had pushed the band into the trees of a canyon where the machine could not go. But the third time it had not worked. Before he could react a second machine appeared out of nowhere and the two angled on the band and forced them into a panicked race across the flat. The stallion had tried to turn them but men on horses suddenly appeared screaming and waving and he was cut off from his band. The filly last saw him galloping into a deep ravine with many men close behind.

The machines were like flying thunder, and fast. The band was terrified and without their stallion they were racing wildly in complete disarray. One young foal fell and was trampled as the herd was churned into a small canyon and suddenly locked up behind metal bars. Squeezed. Nowhere to go. Eyes wide. Nostrils flared. Petrified. Flailing at nothing, and at each other.

The buckskin filly reared and searched for her mother who was with another group being pushed deeper into the canyon. The filly had never been without her mother. Never. She began to thrash and scream trying to get to her. Suddenly bars were closing around her, isolating her from the other horses. Squeezing her until she could no longer move. Such fear she had never known. There were needles but she barely felt them because the fear had such control. She was unable to move at all. She bellowed for her mother.

"No babies for you for a while," a man said.

Then suddenly she was free. Racing with a group of other young fillies. Machines in the air were chasing them. She stopped to look for her mother but a machine was coming straight at her. The filly turned and ran like the wind.

Only she and one other made it into the canyon and into the trees. She didn't know what had happened to the others. Or where they might be. All the filly knew was that she had never felt so alone. Like she was being crushed inside.

She wanted to go look for her family but knew she dared not leave the trees. And she didn't for a very long time.

11

Here We Go Again

It was March 17th.

St. Patrick's Day.

We had been on the road for hours. All spent trying to come up with the right name for our new pregnant mustang. Kathleen had gone for the obvious and Googled things Irish. *Every*thing Irish! Irish names, Irish music, Irish towns, Irish saints. Even Irish food.

Nothing clicked.

Apparently our girl wasn't meant to wear green.

The trip was taking longer than expected. Two separate wrecks on the freeway driving through Birmingham had piled up traffic for miles.

About the time that we broke free of the second one Kathleen and her iPhone began to nibble at the edges of color. Our mama-to-be was Palomino.

Things golden.

Kathleen slipped back more than thirty years to the summer after her first year of law school spent as an intern in Singapore. At the end of the summer she went home with a collection of recipes for dishes she had enjoyed while there and planned a food fest for friends and family. One of the recipes called for the deep golden spice saffron. She remembered it well because she ultimately had to toss out the recipe. The spice was so expensive she couldn't afford it.

"Really??" I said. "Why?"

"Exactly what I wanted to know. I couldn't whip out my iPhone and Google it back then so I actually went to the library and looked it up. When I say it was *expensive* I mean out-of-sight expensive! I was desperate to know why."

She found the answer. Saffron must be harvested carefully by gentle hands because it is very delicate. The process is time consuming, therefore expensive.

Saffron, it turned out, is the spice of kings, one of the rarest, costliest spices on the planet because of the care necessary during harvesting. Certainly, even at the BLM, we had recognized that we were with a very rare young lady. And her relationship would be harvested by the most gentle of hands.

The spice saffron is also therapeutic and has been used for its medicinal and therapeutic values since at least 7000 years before Christ. If you should doubt our new girl's therapeutic value the silly grins we've been wearing since we discovered her should be evidence enough. And like the spice, her equine species goes back way before history was recorded.

"What do you think?" Kathleen asked.

"Saffron," I mused aloud. "I like it."

So did Kathleen.

At the next fuel stop I introduced Saffron to her new name. She was spread-legged, covered in nervous sweat, and had not eaten even a nibble from the hay net. What I didn't realize until later was that she was probably trying desperately to *not* have her baby until her surroundings stopped moving and swaying.

We backed into the front paddock of our barn around 6:00pm. Saffron walked calmly, even curiously out of the trailer and strolled right into the adjacent paddock which would be her home until she delivered. Kathleen and I leaned on the rail and just grinned at her for over an hour, then finally went up and fed the dogs, cat, and ourselves. Then instead of catching up on work undone for two days Kathleen looked at me. I looked at her. And we both said, "You want to?" And off we went back to the paddock by the barn. To stand and grin for another hour. Finally I could stand it no longer and had to go into her paddock and plop down on the bales of straw placed there for that purpose. In a mere matter of minutes – well, okay it was probably thirty minutes or so - she was eating hay out of my hand! After nine-hours in the trailer, now in a strange place, with strange people! And strange horses peering at her across the fence. An unhandled mustang only months out of the wild. I couldn't believe it. The apparent connection Kathleen captured on video at the BLM must've been for real. I was giddy!

Of course at 10pm there was no sun, and no movie lights at the barn, so the ending bite you can see on the *Here We Go Again* video on The Soul of a Horse Channel on You Tube was actually filmed the next day.

It took 19 days for Noelle to take a bite of her favorite feed from her favorite bowl in my hand. It took about four hours for Saffron to take hay from my hand.

Wasting time was not high on her list.

Noelle gave birth 16 days after starting to "bag up".

Miss Saffron took less than four.

On the morning of her fourth day with us she had her baby around 8:00am. We know the time because there was no baby at 7:20am when Kathleen drove off to work at her new passion, teaching American Literature to 11th graders at the renowned Webb School in Bell Buckle. But there *was* a baby when I went down to feed around 8:30am. A mere three and a half days after that nine hour trailer ride! When Kathleen got my photo-text she bundled up her class in a school van and immediately took them on a field trip.

Miss Firestorm was conceived in the wild last April – believe it or not on my birthday if gestation was exactly eleven months. This new little mustang was named Firestorm because that's what she will be brewing for the benefit of horses everywhere. And because she appeared to have a funnel cloud emblazoned on her face :). We call her Stormy.

During that first hour after Firestorm's birth there were warnings in the air from Saffron. I relaxed, pressed hard to keep the adrenaline down, and let baby make the choice to approach, hoping she would wonder what that weird gangling object perched on the hay bale might be. I just sat. And sat. And waited. But truth be known I was enjoying the watch time, mesmerized at what God and Mother Nature had created. A brand new baby, fresh from the womb, who was already walking, and thinking, and eating. Hopping and playing. And definitely curious. I had read the evolutionary logic about this phenomenon but seeing it first hand only moments after she was born brought it all to life in a manner that no book could. Being prey animals, flight animals, the horse in the wild must be on the move immediately; they must hit the ground running so to speak. This baby couldn't wait around for months or years like a human baby, or even weeks like a puppy or a cat (all predators). No, she has to be able to move out with the herd virtually immediately to travel the 8-20 miles a day horses will travel in the wild searching for food, water, and staying away from predators. And Mother Nature had made sure it was so. If she hadn't we would've never heard of the horse. And for those who don't want to spend the time studying the scientific proof that the wild horse and the domestic horse are genetically identical this baby should be proof enough. Because those genes have no idea whether she was born in a paddock in middle Tennessee or out in the wild. And the same is true with every "domestic" foal. They are all born virtually on their feet, thinking, moving, working that brain and body, and ready to go wherever the herd needs to go.

They are all born wild.

And they are born curious as if their brain is reaching out saying *Fill me up! I wanna know things!*

It wasn't long before Miss Firestorm was checking me out. And I began to fill up that new little brain. So she would know things. Good things.

Saffron was no longer wary and seemed to have no issues with me touching her baby. So long as I was sitting on that hay bale. No standing. I was able to rub and scratch Firestorm (imprint her) all over in two separate sessions on her first day of life. And the same again on her second day. All while mama munched hay at my feet. Every once in a while Saffron would stop chewing and focus on what I was doing but not one time did she seem to be upset about any of it. Which I read as a pretty terrific sign as it relates to trust.

I was putting fingers in baby's ears, and mouth, rubbing down her legs, tail and butt. Picking up her feet and she even gave me a wee tiny lick on my ear that first day. But it all had to be done sitting on that hay bale. Saffron felt safe as long as I was a short human. Meanwhile she was giving every other horse in the herd a big *what for* any time they attempted to poke their heads across the fence. I think she even intimidated Noelle.

Throughout her first week with us the most amazing things happened. Barriers crumbled and fell. We've been told that even mares who have grown up in domestic care can be so protective that their babies cannot be touched for days or weeks; and that to imprint a new foal the baby *must be* separated from the mom. Stormy's arrival came so much earlier than expected we were in no way prepared to safely separate mom from baby so I just sat on the hay bale and waited. It was less than two hours after she was born when I was able to begin Dr. Robert Miller's imprinting process.

With no complaints from mom. Every day after that, I reached a little further and stretched the envelope, all with mom's amazing show of trust and approval. Our experience with Noelle did not prepare us for this lady.

Kathleen and I began the ritual we had started with Noelle after Malachi died. We called it No Agenda Time. The purpose, then, was simply to give Noelle some companionship (she was not yet out with the herd), some compassion, because we missed Malachi as much as she did. We would go into Malachi's playpen, open it up to Noelle, scatter a bit of hay around our feet, then sit there and talk paying no attention to Noelle whatsoever. It yielded some of the best moments we've ever had with Noelle. Before or since.

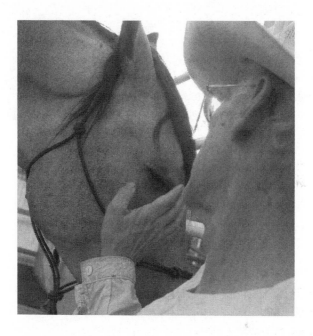

We began No Agenda Time with Saffron and Stormy almost immediately and, again, the yield was just amazing. Every evening Saffron munched hay barely two feet away from us with no apparent worries at all. While her baby was all over both of us. She got lots of rubs and scratches and feet picked up, all without a blink from mom. No Agenda Time proved to be one of the very best things that could've happened to our relationship with Saffron. On various occasions, she reached up and sniffed both of my knees... and my gloves... and more than once asked for a breath exchange.

She had never been so forward. This was exciting. She was exploring. Getting more and more comfortable. But she had not made the choice yet. She was inching up on it. Getting ever closer. But not there yet.

There was a time, not too long ago, when I could not have resisted trying to push the envelope. Reaching out, trying to touch her. Forcing myself on her. But I sat on my hands, figuratively speaking. Because the moment of Join Up had not yet occurred.

It wasn't easy.

I know I tend to say some things over and over but this is so important. *Relationship First* continues to be the key. And the relationship is not set until the horse makes the choice, of her own free will, to say *I trust you to be my leader.* And that's when everything changes for the better.

Why did I choose No Agenda Time rather than a formal Join-Up in the round pen? All I can say is that instinct was in control. Noelle had shown us the way. And like Noelle, Saffron had prior experiences. We wanted to wipe that slate clean, and do nothing whatsoever with her that could generate fear. Which is the net gain from spending such an enormous amount of time with the horses. Letting them be my teachers. Learning intrinsically who they are and what they need. Stuff you just can't get from books and DVDs.

The only sad note to it all was that often Noelle would stand outside the paddock, her eyes locked on Saffy and the new baby, looking very pensive.

Maybe I imagined it but she seemed to be saying *That's supposed to be me.*

Miss Saffron had eaten often from my hand, but only when I was sitting on the straw bale or in a chair. That was her comfort zone. Whenever I would stand she'd get nervous and pull away, but one morning she actually walked up behind me as I was placing hay into her tub and asked for a bite. I held out a handful, very casually with an over-the-top dollop of nonchalance, and she took it without a blink. I could feel another silly grin sneaking across my face.

With all the good stuff going on I felt it might be time to wrangle Stormy into my lap for the first time. This is such an important step, emphasized so much by Allen Pogue in his videos on Foal Training 1 & 2. When the foal relaxes in your lap, even naps, the bond takes giant steps forward.

When Stormy strolled up to say *good morning* I rubbed her, encircling her chest and butt, and pulled her onto my lap. She wriggled and struggled for a moment. Saffy looked up and snorted. I tensed. But baby quickly relaxed. I folded her legs into a fetal position and she dozed off. Saffron returned to munching hay.

When Stormy blinked herself awake, I released my hold on her but she made no attempt to get away. Finally I un-folded her feet and placed them back on the ground. Still she chose to stay. I had to ease my body forward to place her weight back on her feet. She shook and wandered off for a bit of breakfast. Then was immediately back for more rubs. She was in my lap at least once a day for several weeks. Until she simply got too big to fit. On more than one occasion she slept so soundly that she actually snored.

All of this was just extraordinary. Exhilarating. These two incredible new charges.

Wild mustangs.

I had to keep reminding myself.

12

LIVING WITH WILD HORSES

Pete Ramey is my hero for all that he has done and continues to do for the horse. He arguably knows more about the inner workings of a horse's hoof than anyone on the planet. Pete and his wife Ivy took a week-long trip into wild horse country to see first hand, for themselves, if all the reports and research they had read about wild horse lifestyle, and hooves, and health, and happiness were true. As Pete says, they were blown away. This is their story, in Pete's words, and I promise you will be blown away as well:

After all these years, my family and I made our first trip to see the wild horses of the western United States. My work has been dramatically influenced and inspired by the study of these horses and their hooves. The reason I waited so long to go there and see for myself, was I thought that by studying the works of others I had picked up most of the information I needed.

I was first, and most influenced by the work of Jaime Jackson. He paved the way for an overwhelming number of us to learn how to forge healthy bare hooves and dramatically improve the health and performance of domestic horses.

With this came the ability to unlock the mysteries of founder, navicular syndrome, white line disease, and hoof wall cracks. I later studied the wild horse research of Gene Ovnicek and Dr. Robert Bowker. I picked up more information from their work, and valuable confirmation of what I had already learned from Jaime.

So, I walked into wild horse country thinking that I was on a tourist trip; confirming what I already knew. I could not have been more blind. I could not have been more wrong. They were much, much more than I had ever imagined. What I write here, will probably sound very similar to what my predecessors have written. I don't know if anyone's words can get the point across to the world, but I have to try. I thought I was ready, but what I saw literally blew me away. I have worked on thousands of horses, all over the world. I spent six years of my life in the saddle from daylight till dark. I've had the privilege of working on some of the finest horses, for the finest horsemen in the world. Understand that after two minutes with the wild ones, I knew that I had never seen a true horse. I literally had no idea of their potential.

The country was solid rock; mostly baseball-sized porous, volcanic rock that you could literally use as a rasp to work a hoof if you wanted to. Every foot or so, a basketball sized rock was thrown in for good measure. Horse tracks were fairly rare, because there was so little dirt between these rocks. There were a few muddy areas from the recent snow melt, but they were littered with rocks as well. The horses made no attempt to find these softer spots to walk on. They had been walking mostly on snow all winter, so if ever the hooves are soft, tender and poorly shaped, it would be this time of year. I think it was the most critical time to see the horses.

Ivy and I observed, videoed, and photographed at least sixty horses. All of them, from the foals to the aged horses moved effortlessly and efficiently across this unbelievably harsh terrain. They were doing collected, extended trots across this obstacle course that would shame the best show ring work of any dressage horse, with their tail high in the air and their heads cocked over their shoulder looking at us!!! I have never known a horse I would attempt to ride in this terrain. We had to literally watch every step. On the third day we got a half inch of snow (as if we weren't having a difficult time already). We could barely walk at all. It was exactly like trying to walk in a slimy, rocky stream bed. The movement of the horses was not effected by the slippery dusting of snow on the rocks. In fact, they got around much better than the mule deer and the pronghorns. The only animal I saw that rivaled the pristine fluidity of their movement was a lone coyote. The entire time we were there, we did not see a limp, or even a "give" to any rock, or a single lame horse and not one chip or split in any of their hooves. It was an unbelievable sight.

The area we were in had been under heavy snow until a few weeks prior to our arrival. The horses were eating tiny green shoots of new grass emerging from the cracks in the rocks. They would find about one nibble, among the rocks, per two steps. Our calculations confirmed they were, in fact, moving at least twenty miles per day in this rugged landscape. Interestingly, there were a few areas under wooded sections that had decent stands of grass and soft, wet footing, but it was rare to see any sign that a horse had been in there. They preferred the open spaces and high, rocky ridges where they could see around them. The mares were dropping foals while we were there and both the mares and the foals were extremely healthy. What in the world did they eat all winter? The grass would have been covered with snow, if it existed at all. I assure you I will find out next winter!

These horses were all visions of health, but this soon after the snow melt, they should look their worse, I would think. I can't wait to see the same horses in the summertime. I will do that, too.

One day, we took a road trip to a BLM holding facility. Some of the horses there had arrived from the wild only six weeks ago. We were eager for the opportunity to get some close-up photos of them, but they were not even remotely similar to their brothers and sisters in the wild. The care of the horses at the facility was great, by domestic standards; in fact it was exactly what I recommend at home. They were kept in herds, with clean, dry, hard packed footing, and were fed free choice grass hay. They had "plenty" of room and reason to move. I would consider it a perfect spot to rehabilitate a foundered horse. In spite of this, the glow, the vigor, the energy and the startling health was gone, and so were the perfect hooves.......... After only six weeks of domestication in what I would've considered a "natural boarding" situation, the spell was broken. There were nice horses there, don't get me wrong, but they were only shadows of their former selves. The magic was gone. This proved to me beyond all doubt that these "magical creatures" are not a "super breed" or a separate, genetically selected species. It is the diet, the environment and the movement alone that makes them so special.

In the wild, most of the horses react to human presence just like a deer. They run and try to circle downwind, so they can smell you and so you (the predator) can't smell them. Their personalities vary, with some in a herd always a bit curious and some horrified by us. We quickly found that if a curious member of the herd happens to be the leader, the herd is much easier to get close to. Ivy would advance and retreat with these herds, and then sit quietly until they approached her. The first time she did that, the herd stallion circled her, charged up with nostrils flared and blowing, then squared up on her only fifteen feet away. She bowed her head and assumed a very submissive stance. He stood there supercharged for battle, with every vein under his skin visible. From three hundred yards away I could see and feel Ivy vibrating with an even combination of exhilaration and raw terror, but she just sat there, looking small and vulnerable; pretending to graze. The bold stallion soon decided she was no threat and started grazing beside her. After that, I could pretty much bumble amongst the herd and take pictures and observe at will. I have always been deeply impressed by Ivy's horsemanship. It has helped me on many levels, but I would soon find out that we know even less about the communication and training of horses than we do the diet and the hooves!

The horses seem to use drainages, tree lines, and even roads to identify their territories. Large "stud piles" of manure mark these lines. The road we drove in on was no exception (not one vehicle traveled it while we were there, so it came across as a natural feature, I guess). It was lined with these "markers". A young, lone stallion crossed the road one day, and headed toward a small herd managed by the oldest stallion we saw on the trip. The old stallion raced out to meet the young one. We expected a fierce battle, but got much more. They squared up, arched their necks and sniffed noses. The old stallion squealed once and struck out at the air with one foot. They then went shoulder to shoulder in a brief shoving match that ended when the younger stallion took one step backward. Both horses then turned together and ran side by side, ¼ mile back to the road. When they got there, they stood together for a moment, with no signs of friendship or malice. Then the old stallion suddenly wheeled around and galloped back to his herd. The young one just stood there alone on the boundary and watched him go, then turned and ambled back the way he had come. It was as clear as a bell. The old man had said, "Here is the property line, and you were on the wrong side of it. There are plenty of horses over there on that side that will just love you."

Can you imagine a horse standing all alone while the only horse for miles ran away, just because he was rather politely asked to??? I can't, but my family and I saw it with our own eyes! We were able to approach that herd as well. The old man had three old mares, and a brand new foal. The age really showed in this one band with grey muzzles and scarred hides, but they were still completely healthy and able. The old man allowed the mares and the foal to graze very close to us, but always he stayed between us and his little herd.

It has been debated whether mares or stallions lead the herds. In the groundbreaking book 'The Natural Horse",

Jaime Jackson reports that the mares are usually in total control of the herd. To me, it appears to happen both ways. Most herds are definitely run by a lead mare. The stallion seems to be a worthless decoration tailing along behind with little purpose. These boss mares run away with their herd following at the slightest hint of danger. The stallion is never in the lead. Other herds seem to be definitely controlled by the stallion. These monarchs are the most fun to watch. They politely push the herd from behind or sometimes step in front and everyone follows. They will arch their necks and rush between the herd and any deer, antelope, horse or person that happens by; until they are sure there is no danger. These herds seem to be much more relaxed and stable. I'm sure there is always a dominant mare in these herds, but she will be hard to spot. There is almost no ear pinning or pushing each other around. It is the vision of comfort and harmony and the youngest of foals feels safe beside all of the horses in the herd including the stallion.

How has the horse world ignored the remarkable lessons the natural horse has to offer us? Only a few people have noticed them and very little time has been spent studying them. Yet the tiny peeks of a few people have revolutionized hoof care, taught us to cure "incurable" disease and advanced the training world by leaps and bounds. What if real scientific study was done? Who knows what we could learn. Do they deworm themselves? Do they seek minerals and medicinal plants? Do they colic? Do they founder? How old do they get? How long are they sound? How are these mares so healthy right after foaling and a harsh winter? What exactly wrecks their bodies so much after only six weeks of domestication? What if a racehorse was raised in this environment? A steeplechaser? A barrel horse? An endurance horse? A hunter? Would it even be fair to the competition? The list of possibilities goes on and on. The true wild horse is an endangered species, because true wild horse country is almost gone. We had better learn to treat them as such and get all of the answers we can from them before it's too late.

The world has been shocked and amazed by the "natural hoof's" ability to boost equine performance and treat "incurable" hoof disease. I don't want to diminish these facts, but I now I realize we have still set our standards and goals much too low. We haven't even scratched the tip of the iceberg. We can offer our horses much, much more, and will be rewarded by "super-horses" capable of performance, endurance and longevity beyond our wildest expectations. As for competitive performance, the first players in each area of competition to figure this out will be at an unfair advantage. After that, when everyone else follows suit, all of the advantages will be for the horse!!! – *Pete Ramey*

I so want to thank Pete and Ivy for taking the time to write about their experiences with Mustangs in the wild. As I digested the account, I couldn't help asking myself this question: Could I have done what Ivy did when the wild stallion charged her?

Could you?

As scary as it might be I think it says a great deal about how we think about horses and how much we have actually learned from our own. Do I truly believe all I say about the language of the horse, about how they feel and react to things, and whether they are without a cruel bone in their body as the New York Times said. Do I really *believe* that everything changes when the horse, of his own free will, makes the choice to trust you. Have I experienced these things first hand?

Yes I do and yes I have.

So I would have to say yes I would do what Ivy did, probably not without a short prayer, but I would do it in a heartbeat. I truly love that story and I tell it often. Because in one little nugget of time it tells you everything you need to know about the horse.

Every horse.

Read more of Pete Ramey at www.hoofrehab.com

13

CUT TO THE CHASE

I cannot conceive of a reason good enough to mercilessly round up those horses that Pete and Ivy visited for a week in the wild. To disrupt their familes. To splinter and separate them. And to take them from their native homes forever.

But that's what the Bureau of Land Management (BLM) is doing all across the west.

Your government at work. Breaking the very law that Congress charged them with enforcing. All so they can lease the land provided by law to the wild horses and burros to giant corporate cattle ranches. Land that by law is supposed to be managed as a "natural ecological environment. Principally for the wild horses and burros."

Instead it's being managed as a huge cattle ranch where cattle and sheep outnumber wild horses 150 to 1. Cattle and sheep in such large numbers that any semblance of a natural ecological environment is vanishing fast and in some cases has already vanished.

And when the cattle ranchers complain to the BLM that those pesky wild horses are eating too much of the available forage the BLM bows politely and deprives another group of horses the right to live where the Congress of the

United States voted unanimously to allow them to live forever.

Ginger Kathrens and her motion picture cameras have followed the life of the very popular Cloud since the day he was born – the day she named him – more than eighteen years ago. Across those years she has filmed three incredible PBS Specials about Cloud and his herd of mustangs living in the wilds of northern Montana. The latest one *Cloud: Challenge of the Stallions* is truly the best film about wild horses that I ever hope to see. Ginger and The Cloud Foundation are dedicated to the preservation of wild horses on public lands, and the protection of Cloud's herd in the Arrowhead Mountains of Montana and both she and the Foundation have been at the forefront of numerous lawsuits against the BLM for roundups that violate The Wild Free-Roaming Horse and Burro Act of 1971 which the BLM is charged with enforcing. Ginger also spends a great deal of her time filming, documenting, and writing about the cruel, inhumane, and illegal roundups performed by the BLM against the few mustang herds remaining in the wild. At this writing there are more than 50,000 wild horses in BLM holding facilities costing taxpayers more than more than $40 million a year.

The following is Ginger Kathrens' account of a typical BLM roundup, this one in central Utah in early 2013:

I still wake up with the desperate cries of the bay mustang colt ringing in my ears. He was captured on the third day of the roundup of the Swasey Mountain mustang herd near the central Utah farming community of Delta in February of 2013. I hate going to roundups but feel compelled to document the plight of the remaining mustang families in the West. The bay colt's story is only one among thousands.

Despite 16 inches of snow 48 hours before the roundup began, the BLM was committed to starting on schedule. As snowplows opened dirt roads closed by deep drifts, I spoke with the BLM's Contracting Officer's Representative (COR) who cited "contractor availability" as the reason for scheduling the first ever winter roundup of the Swasey.

It was also the stated reason for proceeding with the operation as scheduled despite unfavorable conditions. *What about the wild horses*, I thought? *Why isn't their welfare the most important consideration?*

The next morning we followed the tail lights of a caravan of vehicles driving to the trap site 50 miles from Delta. Temperatures hovered just above zero. *Surely they won't run horses in these conditions*, I thought, remembering the long ago words of Emmett Brislawn whose legendary Wyoming family started the Spanish Mustang Registry. Under Emmett's supervision, I taught my little grullo weanling, Flint, to lead (not to be confused with the still wild Flint of the Pryors). Temperatures at his ranch hovered around freezing and the wind picked up when he quietly walked up to Flint and me. "*Let's call it quits*," he said. As I took Flint's halter off he gave me some advice, "*Never work your colt in the cold. It's just too dangerous. If he gets sweaty, he could get sick.*"

I looked up at the temperature gauge on the Durango. It read 6 degrees. *The BLM will at least delay the roundup*, I thought. How wrong I was. In the pre-dawn cold, at the base of a rocky hill, a BLM officer stood with around 20 of us and went over the observation rules. When he finished I stepped forward. "*We want to go on record as protesting this operation*," I said.

I underscored the danger of running the mustangs in deep crusty snow for miles in cold temperatures with "peak foaling time" only 2 months away. I told him that "*contractor availability*" should not be driving their decisions. The Officer listened politely, dismissing the questions and complaints of other advocates in the crowd. He told us that "*horse body condition*" was the reason for proceeding. If the horses were left out here, he implied, they could die. Ah, the *starvation* card. I wondered when it would be played. BLM was "rescuing" the wild horses from the dangers of living wild. What a disingenuous excuse and what a dodge of the real reason for a winter roundup.

Along with other observers, Lauryn and I climbed the high hill and set up our cameras. I could hear the ominous drone of the distant helicopter—a sound I have grown to despise.

On day one 97 horses lost their freedom and their families. The capture corral looked as if it was on fire, steam rising from the sweaty, exhausted bodies of the mustangs. One cameraman said he thought his lens had fogged up. Then he realized it was steam rising in clouds from the bodies of the horses.

All day long the BLM "tweeted" that the temperature was 32 degrees. My water bottle froze in my backpack. Another observer held a partially frozen Coke bottle in his hand. The thermometer on our car read 16 degrees. Still,

BLM personnel insisted, *the temperature is 32 degrees.* They also insisted that the steam rising from the mustangs in the capture corral did not relate to the amount they were sweating!

This is a 120,000 acre Herd Management Area, a place legally designated "principally but not necessarily exclusively" for the wild horses. Despite these words in the Wild Horse and Burro Act, over 5,000 sheep and 50 head of privately owned cattle are allocated 87% of the forage even though their owners pay virtually nothing for this privilege. With only 13% of the forage allocated for the mustangs, their numbers must be drastically reduced. *How unfair is this? And how costly for the American taxpayers, who foot the bill not only for the privately owned welfare livestock, but also for the lifetime incarceration of our native wild horses.*

We could see for miles, yet we were close enough to the trap to see the horses and to hear their calls. From this distance, I could feel their panic. I can't imagine how anyone could watch this kind of cruelty day after day without suffering untold nightmares. No amount of skill can mask the cruelty of running wildlife with a helicopter. There is no way it can be anything but cruel and inhumane.

On the third day, the first band to be rounded up was small—a bay roan stallion, his two dun mares, and a solid bay foal. Although they weren't as brightly colored as many of the horses on the Swasey Mountains, all four displayed outstanding conformation and excellent body condition. The wranglers waited for the small family to settle down before placing the bay foal in a smaller pen next to that of his parents. Despite being separated, the foal gradually calmed down, finding comfort in standing near his family.

The drone of the helicopter broke the relative quiet. I could see the chopper far away on a nearly unbroken sea of white below the mountains. Lauryn pointed out the distant dots below the chopper. A large band of horses were running for their lives. When they drew closer, we could see a gray mare in front, breaking trail in the deep snow and even deeper drifts. She did not falter, doing what her job had likely been for years. She was the family's alpha female—the lead mare.

I was distracted watching the wranglers separate a cremello foal from the grey mare's family. I didn't notice that the bay colt's family had been loaded into the front compartment of a trailer. Then they loaded more adult horses into the second compartment. Instead of putting the bay colt in the back compartment so he could ride safely with his parents, they loaded three adults from another band in back. The colt called and called, and his mother answered, but the trailer pulled away without him. The colt kept calling and circled the pen, looking for a way out. He charged the fence, launched his body in the air, but fell backwards, failing to clear the six-foot barrier.

He called again and I could hear his mother answer as the trailer drove away. I agonized with the foal as he continued to whinny for his family. *What incredible cruelty*, I thought. In an instant his life changed forever.

Finally, the wranglers loaded the cremello foal and the bay colt into the open back compartment of the long trailer and drove away. I could hear the colt whinnying for his mother even as the horse trailer disappeared over the distant, white horizon.

I know the beautiful, little bay colt has virtually no chance of adoption. Thousands of colorful paints and pintos, palominos and buckskins, duns and grullas are available for adopters to choose from. The bay colt could live for years in a dirt corral with a four digit, plastic tag around his beautiful neck.

I only know one way to silence his calls, which haunt my dreams. I will adopt the bay colt and we will give him a chance to experience life outside the walls of a dirt prison.

Please help us in our efforts to preserve the mustangs on their home ranges and to prevent the destruction of the beautiful families we witnessed in Utah. Thanks so much.

Ginger has found and adopted the bay colt. Bless her for that. We have tried so hard to give Noelle, Saffron, and Firestorm the best life we possibly can. But for Noelle and Saffron we cannot replace their parents, or their former offspring, their stallions, or the mares, aunts, uncles, and cousins they were living with. At least Miss Stormy was born here. She never knew any of those friends or family and hopefully we and our other herd members have provided her with the good stuff of both without the excruciating memories like those of the bay colt. And for those who think I'm beginning slide too close to anthropomorphism: we do know, from study and science, that horses do remember. Forever. Other horses. And humans. Both the very good ones, and the very bad ones.

For more from Ginger Kathrens about the wild horses and/or to donate to The Cloud Foundation visit this link: http://www.thecloudfoundation.org/

14

SEE NO EVIL

"The BLM has not wanted us to see foals with their feet falling off, broken legs, broken necks, sick horses, animals hot-shotted repeatedly, horses drug on the ground by a rope around their necks, stuck in panels and gates or driven to exhaustion by a helicopter. What we cannot see we cannot act on."

Those are the words of Laura Leigh who, like Ginger Kathrens, has been at the forefront of litigation against the BLM. And who, like Kathrens, has lead a team documenting the atrocities of the BLM round-ups in photos and videos. She heads the Wild Horse Education organization.

Leigh said, "Our attorney Gordon Cowan once said, 'The fastest way to create change is to make the guilty party operate in a fish bowl. This allows the public to 'see' the truth and act on it, creating change.'"

The BLM has spent decade upon decade operating in secret, hiding the dirty truth about what actually happens during a helicopter round up. Hiding the fact that seven horses died during one round up. At another an eyewitness saw a paint horse escape from one of the holding pens after a round up and one of the round-up contractors shot and killed the horse as it was racing away. Shooting a wild horse is illegal for the lay public. Apparently not for BLM contractors. Documents finally obtained from the BLM under the freedom of information act marked "For Internal Use Only" spell out all sorts of vicious cold references to keeping certain pieces of information under wraps and under Congressional radar screens on issues like sending horses from their long term holding pens to slaughter in Mexico, and keeping the press and others away from BLM roundups, withholding information about what happens during roundups and after, and about ignoring needs of the horses, and the way the BLM manages the horses in the wild and determines who gets rounded up and why (under current conditions there is no reasonable "why" *any* wild horses and burros should be rounded up), and about the actual number of horses that remain in the wild (much fewer by every count than the numbers reported by the BLM).

Laura Leigh and her Wild Horse Education organization filed a lawsuit charging the BLM with violating the First Amendment of the U.S. Constitution by not allowing access to press and American citizens to view and photograph the round ups and to see documents relating to same. The BLM lost this lawsuit and appealed. Then they moved the "catch pens" for the round ups onto ranchers' private property to avoid being forced to allow the media and others onto Federal lands to watch and to photograph.

But on Tuesday, April 24th, 2013, a mandate came from the 9th Circuit Court of Appeals in San Francisco that upheld the lower court ruling and that decision has now become "case law" in Leigh's suit.

Before these rulings the public and press were blatantly blocked from seeing and knowing what was happening to America's wild horses and burros. From planning, to the range information, through the roundups and all the way to the animals end destinations, much has been hidden. Laura Leigh's Wild Horse Education opened the doors to the information to create change and the 9th Circuit ruling now has far reaching implications for transparency.

With the new access to information the media will be able to expose whatever needs to be exposed to create real change for fair and equitable management of wild horses and burros.

Leigh's organization has also won the first Temporary Restraining Order against the BLM in the history of the 1971 law, which later turned into a successful Preliminary Injunction. And she has won several other rulings successfully tying the BLM's hands.

Many, many thanks to Laura Leigh for these rulings. They were not easy to come by.

I'm still shaking my head in disbelief that an agency of *our* Federal government can and does break the very law they are charged with enforcing. Brazenly and arrogantly. While charging the American taxpayer more than $65 million a year to do so. If this program were executed as the 1971 Law prescribes there would be virtually no need for a program at all beyond monitoring the horses and burros and perhaps spending a bit of that money on research programs that could benefit all horses everywhere.

If the horses were allowed to live on the lands prescribed by the law, in the natural ecological environment prescribed by the law, there would be no leasing of cattle grazing rights on those specific lands because cattle and sheep, for-profit livestock, do not fit into any possible design of a natural ecological environment.

If the courts would force the BLM to repurchase cattle grazing rights on the lands that by law are to be devoted principally to the horses and burros then the natural predators of the horses and burros (wolves, bears, cougars, etc) would return to the ecological balance that existed before the BLM began to allow the ranchers to kill off the predators because they were eating the cattle and sheep.

Without the cattle and sheep on these lands outnumbering the horses and burros by approximately 150 to 1 there would never be a shortage of food or water and there would be a natural balance between predator and horse (and other wildlife species). Natural selection would re-enter the picture. Which would strengthen future lineages of horses and other wildlife. And there would be no need ever to round up any horses and burros for any reason.

This is what the 1971 Wild Free-Roaming Horse and Burro Act of 1971 prescribes. It was passed unanimously by both houses of Congress. Which I suspect is relatively unprecedented. So it is clear what the Congressional intentions were. And those intentions have been for the most part completely ignored ever since.

Why?

I can only suppose it's because this issue is so far down on the list of what is considered important by the American people and the American media that few people even know wild horses still exist. Much less what's being done to them.

We didn't

Only seven years ago, back when we dove into the world of horses without a horse or a clue, I was completely unaware that there were herds of wild free-roaming horses all across the American west, up and down the barrier islands of eastern seaboard, and in many other places around the world. I suppose I might have remembered something about *Misty of Chincoteague* which I read as a child. But that's about it.

Do wild horses have anything to do with foreign affairs or national security?

Do they contribute to economic growth? Create jobs?

Do they help with American infrastructure? Build freeways? Bridges?

Do they contribute to education? Hmmm... they certainly could I suspect. Especially in the areas of how we all treat each other. Relationships. Trust. But even that doesn't seem to be high on our politicians' list of priorities. Or the media's.

But now we know they're out there. With an evolutionary lineage that goes back some 52 million years right here in our American west. They've made it that long without any help from us and I believe we owe them for what we humans are doing to them now that we've taken charge.

Certainly, I would say, a lot more than we, as taxpayers, owe cattle and sheep ranchers. I'm sorry guys, but seriously why should I as a taxpayer be forced to subsidize (with my tax dollars) the success of your ranching operation. For *your* profit, not mine. I've heard so many of you say in videos and in the news that if you were not allowed to graze these virtually free government lands you would be out of the cattle business. I don't recall ever asking you for a share of your taxes to help me make movies for a profit. I don't think I've ever met a storeowner who has asked the taxpayers of America to provide him virtually free land or a virtually free building on or in which he or she could earn a profit for himself or herself.

When I say *virtually free* it's because the grazing rights being leased from the Federal government (which is *us*) are at rates that are only a small fraction of what the same land would cost the rancher to lease from a private owner. And the amount the rancher pays comes nowhere close to what it is costing the BLM to lease the grazing rights to the rancher. Never mind the $65 million a year it's costing the taxpayer to get the wild horses out of the rancher's way.

And virtually none of that expense would be necessary if the wild horses and burros were allowed to remain free with their families and bands on the lands and under the terms granted to them in the 1971 law.

Will this ever happen?

Can it ever happen?

I believe it can.

A few more honest, hard hitting, rulings in court cases against the BLM like Laura Leigh's First Amendment case, and like the case in Colorado in which United States District Judge Rosemary M. Collyer ruled against the BLM forbidding them to remove even one horse from the West Douglas Herd Area in Colorado will, over time, begin to erode the BLM's will and resources to survive on this issue.

And I believe a lawsuit that goes straight to the heart of the BLM's fundamental refusal to enforce the 1971 law as written could bring the BLM to its knees once and for all by forcing the BLM to remove the cattle and sheep from the lands granted to the wild horses and burros and forcing restoration of the natural ecological environment and balance.

The 1971 law outlines everything the wild horses and burros need. There's very little wrong with the law. Other than the fact that the BLM is ignoring the law, actually breaking the law.

Federal Judge Rosemary M. Collyer stated in her ruling against the BLM in the Colorado Wild Horse and Burro Coalition case:

"It is a federal crime to remove a wild free-roaming horse or burro from public lands, convert a wild free-roaming horse or burro to private use, or kill or harass a wild free-roaming horse or burro. Congress delegated to the Secretary of Agriculture and the Secretary of the Interior jurisdiction over all wild free-roaming horses and burros 'for the purpose of management and protection in accordance with the provisions of this chapter.' The Act further provides that "[i]t is the policy of Congress that wild free-roaming horses and burros shall be protected from capture, branding, harassment, or death; and to accomplish this they are to be considered in the area where presently found, as an integral part of the natural system of the public lands. It further provides that "[t]he Secretary shall manage wild free-roaming horses and burros in a manner that is designed to achieve and maintain a thriving natural ecological balance on the public lands" and that "[a]ll management activities shall be at the minimal feasible level . . . in order to protect the natural ecological balance of all wildlife species which inhabit such lands, particularly endangered wildlife species."

These are the same lands where the wild horses and burros are now outnumbered by cattle and sheep 150 to 1.

The Judge goes on to say, "BLM's authority to "manage" wild free-roaming horses and burros is expressly made subject to "the provisions of this chapter[,]" 16 U.S.C. § 1333(a), including the provision that "[i]t is the policy of Congress that wild free-roaming horses and burros shall be protected from capture . . . ." Id. § 1331. It would be anomalous to infer that by authorizing the custodian of the wild free-roaming horses and burros to "manage" them, Congress intended to permit the animals' custodian to subvert the primary policy of the statute by capturing and removing from the wild the very animals that Congress sought to protect from being captured and removed from the wild."

The BLM appealed Judge Collyer's ruling and then abandoned the appeal when they realized that if they lost at the appellate level the ruling would become precedent - *case law* - that could be used against them over and over again in other court actions.

The problem appears to be that many of the lawyers - for reasons I cannot explain - have not been battling the BLM's violations of the law on the merits, often preferring to wage non-explicit emotional law and "poor horse" rhetoric. If we could get all the litigating organizations to fight on the merits of the law that would over time give the BLM so many losses that they'd have no choice but to comply or give up their control, or better yet have it stripped away from them. Consider again the following un-amended language of the 1971 law and what it means:

"It is the policy of Congress that wild free-roaming horses and burros shall be protected from capture, branding, harassment, or death; and to accomplish this they are to be considered <u>in the area where presently found</u>, as an integral part of the <u>natural</u> system of the public lands." Defined as... " the amount of land necessary to sustain an existing herd or herds of wild free-roaming horses and burros, which does not exceed their known territorial limits, and which is devoted <u>principally</u> but not necessarily exclusively to their welfare..."

With no legal basis, 95% of the land that by law was to be "devoted principally" to the welfare of the wild horses and burros was leased to for-profit cattle and sheep ranchers. To the tune of 150 cattle and sheep to one horse or burro. That is illegal.

And that's after the amount of land that was originally designated by congress to be devoted "principally" to the wild horses and burros was arbitrarily reduced by the BLM by approximately 36%. Which also is illegal.

The land on which the horses and burros were to reside, according to the law, was to be "designed to achieve and maintain a thriving natural ecological balance." An impossible task with over a million cattle and sheep on the same land. Which is yet another reason why the cattle and sheep are illegal. Cattle and sheep in no way help to achieve a thriving natural ecological balance.

Forcing proper enforcement of the law would effect the ultimate solution to the problem while drastically reducing the budgets of both federal agencies charged with implementing the protection of wild horses and burros.

Enforcement of the law as written would give the horses and burros the land Congress intended them to have, and there would be little need for "management" or management expenses beyond observation. And perhaps some serious research on how the horse is genetically designed to live, eat, and move. And why.

At this writing, there are more than 50,000 once free-roaming wild horses and burros in BLM holding pens across this country. Less than half that many are still in the wild.

It's called managing for extinction.

And it's wrong.

So very, very wrong.

15

ALONE

The buckskin filly was hungry.

And thirsty.

But she didn't want to move. She was afraid.

So very, very afraid.

She had promised herself that she would never ever be caught again. She would not wait for her elders to react, to tell her something was wrong. Nothing would get by her now. She would run before it was too late. She had lost her father. And her mother. And it was her fault because she had not reacted and moved quickly enough.

And now she was alone.

Only the buckskin and a younger filly had made it into the canyon and the cover of a tall stand of trees. The younger filly was two-colored. Dark black and pure white. All over. The buckskin had not seen a horse like this before. The younger filly wanted to be friends but she was barely a year old, and was always trembling. She needed her mother. And her herd.

The buckskin needed nobody. Ever again.

In human circles a female horse is often called a filly until five years of age, but this buckskin was becoming a mare at less than four. She was growing up. She had no choice.

The commitment and courage lifted her. She stood taller, slowly but with certainty feeling her own strength. Her own will.

And her strength and will were reminding her that she was in need of nourishment. And water. She looked around, more or less seeing the trees for the first time. They were tall and healthy, leaving only the tiniest peeks of blue sky above. She nibbled at a leaf. There had to be some grass around somewhere. She glanced back at the little two-colored filly and her eyes softened. How well she understood what it was like to be afraid. To feel alone.

She turned and began to make her way through the trees to see what she could find. Trees needed water. And water made grass.

The two-colored filly followed, no longer trembling quite so much.

16

SURPRISE SURPRISE

It was April 20th. My birthday.

I had already checked everyone off the list. The kids had called. I had opened my gift from Kathleen. And now I could relax and stop worrying about who was going to pull some wild and crazy thing out of a hat. We settled into our chairs in the paddock in front of the barn for our ritual No Agenda Time. Baby Stormy, now one day shy of a month old, came right up for a rub and a sniff and promptly dropped onto Kathleen's feet for a nap. That, too, was becoming ritual. Miss Saffron was munching hay near our feet, appearing even less concerned than usual about being close to us.

I was doing my best to ignore her, which is what No Agenda Time is all about. But every once in a while, when she would get really close, I'd use that as an excuse to break the rule.

"She wants me to touch her," I might plead. "I can feel it."

"You know the rules," Kathleen would say.

Two fingers onto her cheek for little more than a second was the best I had ever done. Only once. If pressed, she would walk away. If I stood up she would walk away.

The good news was that she wouldn't *run* away like Noelle did back in the beginning. But that same fearful *I-just-can't-go-there* look was in her eyes.

The object of No Agenda Time is to ignore the horse completely until *she* makes the decision to touch, to trust. No matter how it's set up, when the horse decides of her own free will to trust you as her leader everything changes. We usually use Monty Roberts' Join Up to offer that opportunity. But the good things that occurred when we spent No Agenda Time with Noelle after Malachi's death encouraged us to try it with Miss Saffron. She was, after all, a mustang like Noelle. Well, hopefully not *too* much like Noelle. We'd been at it for a month, sitting right here every night, since the day Stormy was born, which was three days after Saffron arrived; and we had decided that once we started we would pay no attention to time. We would take whatever time it took. Especially so because we really enjoyed this opportunity to sit with the horses and talk about our day. And baby Stormy's attention made up for any lack thereof from Saffy.

We hadn't been sitting long on this birthday evening when there was a crunch behind me on the pea gravel covering the paddock. A close crunch. I glanced up at Kathleen.

"Is she close?"

Kathleen's eyes were widening. She nodded.

"Very."

My heart was skipping beats. I wanted so to turn and see. Kathleen was easing her iPhone out of its holster. And suddenly there was this marvelous tickle. Whiskers on my neck. And a warm breath in my ear. Then a rub, cheek to cheek so to speak.

I was frozen in place for a long moment. I didn't want to blow it. Finally I couldn't resist. I turned slowly... and kissed her on the nose. Then reached around and scratched the off side of her face.

"Hello Miss Saffron," I said softly. "Welcome home."

She blinked. And blew me a long slow breath. I returned it.

Kathleen's phone camera was clicking away.

"Happy birthday," she said. "I told her it was today."

My hand began to sneak up her face to the top of her head, sliding over to scratch the base of her ear. A thumb slid inside and rubbed and rubbed. Miss Saffron purred.

I didn't know what to think. The best progress I had ever had with any of our horses was incremental. A little at a time. Even now, four years after Noelle came to us, I could barely touch her ears. And only then on *some* days. I wondered if I should attempt to stand up. My hand slid down her neck, rubbing and scratching as it went. I felt like a school kid on my first date, trying to sneak my hand onto her shoulder.

I scratched back up her neck and eased into a standing position as I went. Saffy took no notice. Suddenly I hit a sweet spot and she responded in ecstasy, stretching, reaching for the sky.

Yes please! More, more!

I scratched all the way down her back to her tail bone, slid down her hip, and underneath to her tummy and her belly button, then back forward, and down her front leg to her hoof. I was tempted to lift it, but probably wisely chose not to. This was enough for the moment. Leave it all positive.

Dropping back into the chair I turned to Kathleen with my mouth gaping open. Saffy rested her chin on my shoulder and actually dozed off.

"I've never seen anything like this," I said. "A few moments ago I couldn't touch her. And suddenly... like she just flipped a switch... she's in.'"

"*All* in," Kathleen grinned. "Like I said. Happy birthday."

Noelle was in her usual spot in the next paddock watching it all. Why, I found myself asking again, was she so different? So *very* different?

The question had badgered us virtually from the time Saffron arrived, for even then we knew. Long before this birthday gift, we had toyed and talked about several obvious probabilities for difference but there was still a big open space of unconnected dots.

Until I began to write about Saffy.

Definitely the difference in ages when each came to us was a piece of the puzzle. And I'm certain that our own maturity played a role. We now had twice as many years with horses than we did when Noelle joined our family and we were pretty much mistake free with Saffy.

But, as I began writing about her, another concept bubbled up, one that I now believe could be a major piece of the puzzle. As mentioned earlier some of the very best moments with Noelle came after Malachi died when we were all so torn apart. The No Agenda Time we spent with Noelle in Malachi's playpen definitely evoked her best efforts ever. She was reaching out, wanting to be close, overriding her hair trigger fear quotient. Even out in the paddock this was true. We felt that she could be on the verge of a Join Up.

And what did she get for crossing all those thresholds?

As with the mistake of the early lead rope, we suddenly scared her to death and for the third time in her life ripped her away from everything she called home. From where her baby had been born. And died.

We moved.

From southern California to Tennessee.

For Noelle it began when the horse transport informed us that there was no way they could get up the hill to our house where the paddocks and stalls were. Too steep and curvy.

The rest of the herd could be walked down the hill to the transport. But not Noelle. She would have to be shuttled down the hill in a smaller trailer. But the only flat ground for loading horses into a trailer was well away from her paddock. And the only reasonable place to load her was out of the playpen. Which would mean she would be on a slant attempting to load uphill into a trailer on a slant.

All things considered she seemed to be dealing with it well and in pretty short order she stepped up into the trailer in pursuit of a slice of tasty green alfalfa. The door swung shut... on her butt... which wasn't quite inside. So it wouldn't latch. She fired her back legs which exploded into the door and sent it and two people flying. She was out in a flash and raced through the playpen into the farthest corner of her paddock. Totally ballistic. Scared to death. Not at all understanding what had just been done to her. Or why.

From that moment it took two and a half hours to ultimately get her into a frame of mind to give it another go. But finally she loaded.

It was a three day trip with a 24-hour rest stop during which Noelle had to remain on the transport for fear they might not be able to get her back on when it was time to leave. And, too, she had not yet been integrated into the herd.

When she finally landed in Tennessee, she was a very different horse. She didn't refuse my touch but she had definitely regressed, was unresponsive, and was way more freaky about every little thing. Which is not really surprising considering the experience from her point of view. Just sad. As the cold weather crept in we decided that it would be cruel to keep her locked up in an isolated paddock during the winter on the hope that we might make some progress. So we turned her out with the herd. There would probably be little work with her anyway since Kathleen was still living in California until the twins graduated from high school and was only back for long weekends every three or four weeks.

Almost four years after the move, barely a week ago, we reinitiated No Agenda Time with Noelle. We sit and talk while she munches hay from a small round tub at our feet. Last evening it was all was quiet and nice until she caught the rim of the tub with her lip and it lifted maybe two inches off the ground. Before the sound of the tub's plop back onto the pea gravel had dissipated Noelle was halfway across the pen.

Still.

We hope we can recapture what we had with her before the move to Tennessee, and take it further. But it will be on her time, not ours. By her choice, not ours. Meanwhile we are thanking God daily for Saffron. And Miss Firestorm. And that very special surprise on the evening of my birthday.

17

BELIEVE

"That first night when you were offering Saffy hay from your hand, your heart was expecting her to take it. I could see that."

It was Kathleen talking. We were still tugging at the differences between Saffy and Noelle.

"You believed it. With Noelle, in the beginning, you didn't believe. You pretty much knew she wouldn't. At best, you were only hoping. With Saffron you were feeling and projecting warmth and trust. With Noelle you were only *thinking* it. That makes all the difference."

She was right of course. I was supposed to know that.

"Still, these are two very different horses."

"I agree," she said. "But you are also a very different person than you were four years ago."

I had to keep telling myself that just a few weeks ago this mustang, fresh from the wild, had never willingly touched or been touched by any human. And now she was saying *I trust you completely. To touch me, rub me, scratch me anywhere. At any time. I will not flinch, I will not pull away. And I will thank you for being here.* And it wasn't just me. She totally trusted Kathleen as well.

I was pinching myself several times a day expecting to wake up and find that we were in a dream, Miss Saffron and me. Some silly figment of my imagination.

A couple weeks after my birthday surprise I was picking up her feet, which I've never been able to do with Noelle. Barely more than a month later Saffy's feet were being trimmed.

Even now she still blows me away. Every day.

And yet, when the time came for me to show Saffy that there was nothing at all wrong with wearing a lead rope I wasn't particularly looking forward to it. The only time a lead rope was ever put on Noelle was an explosive disaster.

But with Saffy, Kathleen had left me no choice.

It was a couple of nights before, just after feeding. We were enjoying No-Agenda Time with Saffron and Firestorm, just chatting away, pretty much ignoring the pair nibbling hay at our feet. Suddenly, without a word, Kathleen bolted out of her chair and strolled over to the panel where Saffy's halter was hanging. Halter-to-be. The halter she had never yet worn. For days I had been rubbing it on her back, legs, neck, and occasionally letting it "slip" across her face. But I hadn't yet dared to attempt to slip it over her nose. She was still worried anytime it got close to her face.

Kathleen snared the halter off its hook and strode calmly and confidently back over to Saffy. *Who is this?* I wondered. Not my fearful ever-cautious wife who still doesn't like to be in the same pen with Noelle. Or even in the tight quarters of the barn breezeway when two or three horses gather. She slowly and methodically began what I would call a classic Monty Roberts or Pat Parelli drill, rubbing Saffy from back to front, top to bottom, with the halter in hand. The perfect approach and retreat, sliding close to her face then backing off to her withers or all the way back to her tail. I was in awe. On and on this went as daylight dwindled into darkness.

You picked this time on purpose! I wanted to say. Kathleen hates to be in front of the camera. The camera which I didn't have with me anyway because all this was a complete surprise. So it was just me and the iPhone. And no light! I clicked away having no idea whether anything other than darkness was landing on the lens.

Finally she began the serious work in earnest. And very soon there it went right over Saffy's nose as smoothly and effortlessly as if Kathleen were haltering her Skeeter.

A complete non-event because: 1) Saffron had first chosen to trust us of her own free will... and 2) Kathleen worked slowly and confidently up to the moment. But it was a threshold crossing for both.

Kathleen had managed to internalize the fine points of keeping her adrenaline down at a moment when, no matter how trusting Saffron had become, this was going to be a first-ever time for that scary horse-eating halter to slide onto her head. That fact alone is enough to send human adrenaline soaring, which in turn will send horses flying. Kathleen knew that, but was able to keep her herself calm, and keep Saffron's trust in place. She slipped the line through the loop but didn't actually tie it, snugging it up for a few moments before slipping the halter off and letting Saffron help herself to a few munchies. Then the entire drill was repeated for good measure. And by now dark was completely upon us.

"That was awesome!" I exclaimed. "Simply extraordinarily awesome!"

"The most amazing part of it," she said, "was that you didn't open your mouth for more than fifteen minutes. Never said a word!"

"I was dumbstruck," I smiled.

She was very calm and relaxed about the entire thing. Until the next morning when she finally exploded with a grand "Eeeee Hawwww!" And did a little dance around the kitchen. How many people get to be the first human on the planet to successfully halter a mustang fresh from the wild.

The next evening the routine was repeated but took much less time. And once again, Kathleen slipped the line through the loop but didn't tie it. Then the next morning – when there was plenty of light thank you very much – she walked right up to Saffy, slipped the halter over her face... Slipped the line through the loop... and tied the knot

I manned the camera.

"Thank you my Sweetie. You've taken a giant step. This horse trusts you implicitly. You're no longer the only the face in front of the camera."

"Now it's your turn," she said, and swapped a lead rope for the camera hanging around my neck.

I had to show Saffy there was nothing wrong with wearing a lead rope… and giving to pressure. A certain image of Noelle kept coming to mind. It wasn't pretty.

But these are two very different horses, I kept telling myself. Saffron trusts us implicitly and has often told us so. But as I clipped the rope onto Saffy's halter neither of us knew that I was about to make a serious mistake.

We all know that mustangs come out of the wild with an enhanced fear factor. They're taught from the day they're born that to stay alive they must be afraid of everything that moves and most things that don't. React first and ask questions later. But Miss Saffy's gift of complete trust on my birthday had apparently lulled me into oblivious folly. I've always taught a horse to respond to a lead rope by letting them teach themselves. Pull the rope just barely taught enough to let the horse be a bit uncomfortable from the pressure. Then hold it until she takes a forward step, which releases the pressure and gets her lots of praise and rubs. Then do it again, and again, and again, until she has the concept well absorbed and leads to a loose line.

That's how Stormy learned to walk on a loose line in two days. But she had never actually lived in the wild. And mama wasn't piling on the lessons in fear because she was no longer freaking out at every little thing. But the minute that lead rope tightened on Miss Saffy she went completely ballistic. Old fears of being confined with nowhere to run leaped to the surface and she started peddling backward across the paddock at light speed, dragging me with her. This was my first "rodeo" and I thought seriously about turning loose and racing for cover more than once. But, inexplicably, I didn't. And I even remember the moment when I realized what was wrong and shamed myself for making the mistake of allowing her to pull on the rope so hard that she felt inescapably trapped. And there were a number of fleeting thoughts about how calm I was as she dragged me all over the paddock. The years with the herd were paying off. I knew as long as I could keep my balance I was in no serious danger. Saffy is sweet, and trusting, and bonded. But she was afraid. A wild horse with three years of experience living with fear in the wild. All of this caromed through my brain in a matter of seconds. While I was desperately looking for a moment to catch up and loosen the line to take the pressure off. It came when she backed onto a small mound of pea gravel and her back feet almost slipped out from under her. The line went slack. I advanced, talking softly and calmly to her, and managed to keep the line loose, hopefully restoring her trust.

"Easy, Miss Saffy. Easy," I whispered, moving ever closer. Her eyes were wide, nostrils flaring, and her breathing was heavy. But I felt confident about her inner self. I believed she would respond. And she did. Her eyes narrowed and her breathing eased. I stroked her forehead, then both cheeks with both hands. She came back to me and I offered her a treat. At first she said *no thanks*, but then had second thoughts and munched it down. I put the tiniest amount of pressure on the lead rope to the left, easing her face around to see another treat in my hand. She responded, and took the treat. Then I moved the line to the right, and again she responded, and took another treat. The halter came off. She got a rub on her face and neck and I walked away, leaving her to think about it.

It was scary, but a good beginning, I thought. For both of us. It was my first such wild and wooly experience and I was happy I stayed with it when I wanted to drop the rope and run. And happy that I got her back and was able to leave the experience positive instead of negative. And I vowed to not let that mistake happen again.

The next morning, happily, with Kathleen available to shoot, Saffron showed no resistance to the halter and lead rope. No bad memories. And I was mentally set to never allow that rope to get tight, to become restrictive, to make her feel trapped or confined.

I thought about Chapter 22 of *The Soul of a Horse*. Cash had gotten his lead rope wrapped around a hitching post and felt suddenly confined. He freaked out and yanked the entire hitching post out of the ground. From that moment, he could never be tied without freaking out. The ultimate solution was Clinton Anderson's Aussie Tie Ring which allows the lead rope to slide through the ring, telling the horse that he can get immediate relief from the pressure of being tied. With the ring, Cash quickly began to realize that he wasn't actually tightly confined and he would relax. We've never tied any other way since.

That would be the procedure for Saffy on this day. The first time I put tension on the line, she wanted to back away from the pressure. I merely let the rope slide through my hands until she stopped, which was almost immediately. Then I held an ever so slightly taut line asking her to take a step forward. She stared at me seemingly forever. I dangled a treat and finally she reached as far as she could reach without taking a step, and I let her retrieve the treat. Then I moved away, getting beyond her reaching range unless she took that all-important first step.

The line went slightly taut. Even though intrinsically I know this stuff works it's still sort of amazing to me when it does. She reached as far as she could reach but it was no longer enough. She thought about it, only for a moment, and then took that first step.

Then another.

And another, her resistance dissolving away, steps coming faster.

We turned several circles in both directions and soon she was walking with me on a completely loose line. We made one more round, with much praise and rubbing, and I removed the halter. This is how I wanted to leave it. With her thinking about following that loose line. My teeth were clenched down tightly on the enormous *EeeeHawww* trying to escape. This was, after all, a pair of all-time firsts. The first time this wild mustang had ever taken forward steps on a halter and lead rope... and the first time ever that I had been on the other end of such first steps (except with two babies).

It felt spectacular. But I walked off as calmly as I could. As if it was just the way things were supposed to be.

And guess what? She walked with me into the barn as if we were still attached. Made me wonder why we were messing with that silly ol' lead rope anyway. Oh yeah, now I remember. This horse is a wild mustang.

I wish they could all be like this lady.

Our very special Miss Saffron.

18

THE CANYON

The golden stallion pawed the grizzled rocky earth outside the canyon's entrance. Something didn't feel right.

Behind him the matriarch turned a nervous circle. She was growing impatient. She needed sleep.

Minutes passed. The stallion sniffed the air, then eased closer to the outcroppings that formed the entrance. The herd wanted to follow, but the matriarch spun with pinned ears and stopped them in their tracks.

The stallion scanned the horizon behind him, and sniffed again the breeze blowing lightly at his back. There seemed to be nothing to fear but his senses wouldn't be still. He looked back at the matriarch. A look she well knew. *Do not follow. Wait here.*

Once inside there was only one way out. The stallion's herd had been trapped in this canyon before. By humans on horses and several of the herd were lost. It was his job to make sure it didn't happen again.

The stallion would've preferred to turn back but he knew the matriarch was tired, absent her usual spirit, and that convinced him to have a closer look. He walked slowly, quietly, through the outcroppings of the passageway. Behind him, the uneasy herd was squirming and pawing the ground. They could smell the fresh grasses and wanted to go in. The trip had been too far, too long without forage.

Inside, the canyon was at least partially green with grasses following the edges of a crystal clear stream that disappeared underground before departing the small gorge's towering walls. All seemed quiet and as it should be. Then something caught the big stallion's eye. A movement. At the far end. Another horse was emerging from a stand of trees. Followed by a second smaller one. They were nibbling at the grass along the water's edge. A buckskin, and a young filly, two-colored like a colt the stallion had sired himself. The stallion made no sound but the buckskin at the far end soon sensed a new presence and looked up.

Eyes met.

Neither moved for a long moment. Then the stallion exhaled a relaxing snort and tossed his head. The buckskin cautiously returned it, but inside she wanted very much to race to him kicking up her heels.

19

WILD BABY

There is only one Daddy's girl in our herd.

Only one who was sucking on my finger before she was three hours old.

Only one who still does all those things with me she did in her first few days on the planet. Except go to sleep in my lap. Thankfully.

She will always be special. And if for some reason we were separated and reunited ten years later there is no question that we would pick up right where we left off. That's the way it is with the bond.

Is Firestorm happier here than she would be in the wild? There is, of course, no way to answer that. But I hope so. That's certainly our goal. What about Saffron? Again, I cannot say. But I *can* say with certainty that they both enjoy their relationships with humans. Because all of it is based upon their choices. Not without leadership, but the choices, all of them, remain theirs. We lead them but we never force them.

I like to think of our relationships and the things we do together with the horses as opportunities for all of us to experience pleasurable things we would never have the opportunity to experience without having met, without each other. Opportunities to grow. To expand our knowledge base. Like moving from middle school to high school.

Which I believe is why Monty Roberts' mustang Shy Boy came back to him of his own free will when Monty turned him loose in the wild to re-join his own herd. He was gone, off with the herd, all night long. Monty stayed awake most of the night. He had lookouts positioned all over the place with radios, watching for the herd. Around nine o'clock the next morning, a radio crackled and blared that the herd was in sight, headed more or less their way. Shy Boy was out front.

At the bottom of the ridge that separated the horses from Monty's encampment, the herd stopped and Shy Boy climbed to the top of the ridge. He stood for quite some time looking first at the herd, then at the camp. Finally, he turned and galloped down the ridge toward the camp, weaving in and out of tall brush, slowing to a trot, then a walk, stopping only when he was nose-to-nose with Monty. I cried like a baby when I saw that video. Completely lost it. Imagine how you would feel if that was your horse, turned loose to make his own choice, to run free with his herd, or come back to you. You would surely know that you had been doing something right.

I also lose it just about every time I touch Firestorm. Yes, she's acting a bit like a young teenager. But she's still Daddy's girl, and that will not go away. If I act like I'm going to pull her onto my lap she still (at sixteen months) totally relaxes. I'd be flattened of course were I to follow through now but her reactions are the same now as then. She still sits on her beanbag. She comes when called. And just this morning she stepped up onto her little platform… with all four feet! Which is way more difficult now than it was a year ago. Her body is now two feet longer than the platform!

And she's the only horse in our herd about whom I know everything. Every little detail of her existence, right from the beginning.

Stormy was born curious and very bright and I was filling her little brain with good stuff right from the get go. She was only three weeks old when she learned to lead on a loose line.

This took minutes, not hours.

On this same day she had her first sit on her beanbag. Again, it only took minutes. She gets things very quickly.

After the above I had the bright idea to have a sit myself and pull her into my lap. We both would up on the ground.

The funny thing is that I was the befuddled one. Stormy was just fine with it. My lap was already getting a bit small to suit her anyway. There were a lot of firsts that day. She learned to back up, and move her butt left and right. She learned to understand a finger point and move off in that direction. And to step up onto her pedestal.

Unlike Saffy, this is all fully explainable with Stormy. Using Dr. Robert M. Miller's renowned foal imprinting methods, all taken to the next level by Allen Pogue's foal training, each and every one of you can accomplish everything I've accomplished with this little wild horse.

Firestorm was proving beyond any doubt that she is a horse. Not just a mustang, although she is one. Not just a domesticated horse, although she is that as well. But moreover, she's a horse. She and her mama have as strong a relationship with humans as any never-wild domestic horse. And conversely the rest of the herd is proving that any domestic horse allowed to live like horses were genetically designed to live – like the wild horses - will be happier and healthier. And stress free.

In other words, we humans have *not* bred the wild horse out of our domestic charges. The genetics are still the same. We haven't bred away their ability to grow rock solid feet. We have *taken* it away. We haven't bred away their ability to live happy, healthy lives without colic, hoof lameness, ulcers, and stress. We have *taken* it away. But whatever we've taken away is temporary. If we just set them up for success and get out of their way their genetics will give it all back.

Mustangs and Domestics living together as they are all genetically designed to live

Time seemed to fly by. Almost as fast as Miss Firestorm grew. We continued her schooling but she taught herself a lot as well, like in the photo below of Stormy at three months desensitizing herself to a tarp. My kind of training!

At three months

Above: At 3 months – Below: at 16 months

Daddy's girl. She still, at 16 months, walks over after eating, nuzzles up to my ear, and goes to sleep. That's one very special feeling. Actually *two* very special feelings because her mama does the very same.

20

A New Family

The buckskin mare rose quickly through the ranks of her new family and now, just less than three years after she and the two-colored filly were nibbling grass in the canyon, she was already second in command to the matriarch. Virtually a herd leader.

She had survived a roundup. And been ripped away from the safety and security of the only family she had ever known. It would have been excruciating even for a predator. But she was a prey animal, a flight animal. And because her experience was deeper and wider than any in her new family she was trusted.

And she was pregnant. For the first time. Almost three months pregnant.

The shot she was given by the men when she was captured three years before was a temporary birth control drug called PZP, supposed to last for two years. An experiment of the government.

It had worked.

But at last the buckskin was carrying the big golden stallion's foal and she was happy. She knew it would be a special baby. And she would be proud.

The matriarch was also pregnant, but much closer to birth than the buckskin and that too made the buckskin happy for she would be able to observe, and learn.

She felt strongly bonded to her new family and felt very secure under her stallion's watch. He and the matriarch had kept the herd safe, while others around them were not so fortunate.

Still the stallion remained uneasy. Too many things were changing, too quickly. He rarely felt really safe, not like he had in the past. He no longer worried much about big cats and bears and wolves. They seemed to be disappearing. It was the men and thunderous machines that were always on his mind. Hiding from them. Eluding them. Keeping his band safe.

And the grasses were so much harder to find than in times past. Only yesterday they had left the cover of the trees and travelled a long distance to an area that had always been good, always been green, but it was now bare ground. No grass at all. Only the leavings of cows covering the barren earth. They had wiped it bare, left their mark, and then moved on. There was so much the golden stallion didn't understand about all this.

So much.

21

FIRST COLD MORNING

It was the first really cold morning of the fall. At least really cold from the perspective of a southerner. It was 31 degrees with winds at 20 knots plus or minus.

It was cold to me.

And apparently to Noelle. Normally she is the first or second in position for the morning feed. Her place is in the round pen right next to the barn. But on this morning she was standing on the western pasture hillside, maybe 40 yards away from the barn. In the sun. The barn was still in the shade. As was the pasture east of the barn. And the round pen.

I went about the business of closing gates that were necessary to insure that everyone got to eat in peace and then started filling buckets.

"Noelle, come on around! Breakfast time."

She knows the gig. She turned and gazed at me but didn't budge. Everybody else was either in place or on the way.

I went back to the buckets. There were now eight of them after the addition of Saffron, and soon thereafter Miss Firestorm.

I like to have the two adult mustangs isolated before starting to feed because they are the two most dominant horses in the herd and I don't want to risk them straying over to someone else's feed and taking over. Saffy and Stormy were already waiting patiently in the front paddock.

"Noelle, come on! Be a good girl now. Come on."

Nothing.

The wind was picking up and I was getting colder. Should've worn the ski coat.

When I finished filling the buckets she still hadn't moved a muscle. Very unusual. Even strange. I debated whether or not to shut the gates that would exclude her from others' breakfast but she appeared to be carved in stone so I decided to just go ahead and feed the rest and keep an eye out.

Sure enough everyone finished and I was in the Gator headed out to the eastern pasture with the morning hay when I finally saw her ambling past the barn.

She turned the corner toward the round pen where she always eats, and suddenly stopped in her tracks. There were two other horses where she is supposed to eat. She looked up the hill at me and I swear to you she couldn't have conveyed any better with words the hurt and confusion she was feeling.

The look on her face was explicit. As if her entire life was falling apart.

To put this in perspective, Noelle had been the herd leader from the day she walked into the herd three years earlier. Until the day Saffron joined the herd.

On Miss Firestorm's 10-week birthday we decided to see how her mom, Saffron, and Noelle would do sharing a pasture; the goal being to finally get the herd all together as one, all out 24/7 with both pastures to roam. The result was a disaster. Big mistake. You can watch the video *Two Mustangs – Rounds 1, 2, & 3* on YouTube – The Soul of a Horse Channel. It's brutal. Mostly because Saffy simply would not give up, and Noelle kept coming until I broke it up. That was Round One. Clearly too early. Too soon. We now believe that Saffron had more than dominance on her mind. She was worried about protecting her baby.

Back to the drawing board. Or rather back to separate pastures. For the next four-and-a-half months we rotated horses and pastures every day so that both Noelle and Saffy would have time with all members of the herd – except each other – and everybody would get equal time in the east and west pastures. What a logistical nightmare!

But I was seriously worried about Saffron. She is not as, shall we say, stout as Noelle. Doesn't have the butt or the power of Noelle. You can see this on the video. Noelle was getting in two or three kicks for every one from Saffy. All adding up to yet more proof of the already known fact that I will never ever understand how dominance is decided in a herd. Human logic simply doesn't apply.

When we tried again four and a half months later – Round Two - it ended in a stand-off. Or rather a stare-off. We separated them again to let then think about it all and the next day was Round Three. The final round. All eating peacefully together. There were no clues that day which mustang would be dominant but my money was firmly on

Noelle. Again, you have to see Round One to fully understand why.

I was wrong.

Three days later, Saffy was calmly moving Noelle off of
hay piles. I was dumbfounded.

For quite some time I sensed a change in Noelle. A
sense of – I guess you could call it - depression. She would
spend a great deal of time totally away from the herd. Off by
herself. She was much more receptive to my hugging and
rubbing. And she and Saffron's baby began to hang out a lot.

She was in the same sort of funk she seemed to be in
shortly after Stormy was born as she would watch the new
baby frolic and play. And watch us scratching and rubbing
on her. I kept wondering if she was thinking about Malachi.

Over time Noelle began to ease back into the herd and
finally began to spend quite a bit of time off at the far end of
the western pasture with Saffy and Stormy. Birds of a weird
feather, these mustangs.

And the dominance issue still wasn't fully decided.
Then, or even now. There are days when Saffron will approach and Noelle will just wander off, apparently giving to
her. There are other days when Noelle will turn her butt to
Saffy and threaten a kick... and Saffy will be the one to
wander off. Yet, as reported earlier, in close quarters Noelle
will usually give way to virtually anyone taking a stand. Feeling enclosed is not a happy feeling for her when other horses
are around.

Just one more enigma.

Which is possibly one of the reasons man has so often
advocated physical dominance over a horse. Just when you

think you have one figured out, something changes. When the horse is afraid of you, nothing changes. As the old cowboy told me about Mariah, "That horse out there is here for one reason. My pleasure. And I'm going to make sure she damn well understands that."

His statement was probably the deal closer for me. After hearing it I was going to make sure Mariah damn well came home with us. Kathleen was against it. But I planned to convince her no matter how long it took. Which was almost a week, but come home with us she did. And three lives were changed for the better.

So it's been with all eight of our horses. Including those indecisive mustangs.

As to the question of herd leadership my gut feeling from observation is that's it's probably Noelle... *when* she chooses to go to the trouble. When she feels like hassling with it. When she doesn't, she just steps aside and lets Saffron have it. But while these two are tossing it back and forth there could be a storm rising. A cute little filly with an ambitious twinkle in her eye who is growing bigger and stronger and more confident every day.

It could get interesting around here.

22

DEJA VU

The buckskin mare was once again on watch as the matriarch slept under a stand of trees. The two-colored filly, almost a mare herself now, slid up next to the buckskin and looked out toward the sliver of sun just beginning to pry itself over the horizon. The filly nickered softly and the buckskin turned and touched her nose with a gentle breath of air.

They would be moving away from the sun today with very little around to hide them and the buckskin worried about that.

The golden stallion was nudging the matriarch. Better to get going before the sun is too high in the sky. The rest of his little herd was scattered around nibbling on patches of dry grass and the stray tasty weed here and there.

The matriarch left the trees to survey the distant horizon. She knew exactly where she would take the herd today. They were in need of water and there was only one source that remained open and available. Unfenced.

The buckskin knew where they would be going as well, for she understood that it would someday be her job to know.

The thunderous roar seemed to come out of nowhere. From over the trees, the machine was suddenly on them and the little herd scattered in panic running in every direction. It was the same machine that had been after the golden stallion and his band for years and years.

The stallion screamed at his herd and raced back into the cover of the trees. The matriarch followed, and the buckskin, and the multi-colored filly. The others were racing off toward the sun. The machine flew after them. The stallion did not like what he was seeing. Something was wrong. The machine was actually turning the other herd members back toward the trees.

Why would it do that??

His answer came quickly as a band of men on horses appeared behind him yelping and screaming and racing through the trees right for the stallion and his charges.

"There he is!!"

"This time he's ours!"

The matriarch raced out of the trees and down the slope toward open range. Those who didn't follow were gathered and pushed by the stallion as the men got closer and closer. Now the machine was behind them as well.

The stallion surveyed the prairie looking for escape routes. There were none. They would have to split up. The matriarch and the buckskin knew as well what had to be done. They had all done it before, always with success. Suddenly the stallion and several of the band pealed off to the left as the buckskin and the matriarch veered with others to the right. Just as suddenly two more machines appeared out of nowhere bellowing thunder and pushing both bands back to the center.

Three machines!

Never before had that happened!

When the stallion again tried to move off to the left the machine blocking his way sank until its metal feet were almost touching him.

They ran and ran and ran. All of them were tiring. All of them needed water. But the matriarch was rapidly reaching the point where she could run no longer. All she wanted to do was lay down. She was spent.

The stallion was in the rear, where he always stayed, to protect the herd from predators sneaking up from behind. So he saw the matriarch go down. He was running so fast he had to circle back to her and one of the machines was on him before he could finish the circle, flying virtually on the ground, pointing its swiftly rotating blades right at him. He tried to dodge, this way and that, but the machine stayed one step ahead. He could *not* leave her there and he could not get back to her! It was excruciating! Unbearable!

More men on horses appeared in front of them waving sticks at them, directing them between two barriers that narrowed and closed in on them until every horse was surrounded.

Except the matriarch.

The buckskin could not believe she had allowed this to happen again! She and the multi-colored filly made their way to the stallion's side. He was thrashing at two men with whips swinging at him. Then suddenly he bellowed to the sky! A third man had hit him with a stick of fire that almost paralyzed him. A pain like he had never felt before shooting through his entire body. He was having trouble keeping his balance.

"You ain't such a big deal anymore are you?!"

The golden stallion was removed from the others and put into a pen by himself. The rest of the herd bellowed and screeched in emotional agony. No stallion! No matriarch! And a colt only three months old had vanished from the herd. The buckskin had seen the matriarch go down but had not missed the colt until now.

Much later that night, nearing dawn, the stallion stood by the seven-foot barrier separating him from the herd softly nosing the buckskin. He liked her a lot. Liked her spirit. Liked the way she had helped him and the matriarch keep their herd from capture untold times. But there was nothing he could do for her now. Nothing he could do for any of them. Except himself.

The elegant stallion nuzzled the buckskin one last time and turned toward the barrier separating him from the open desert. He reared and ran straight at it, lifting himself with every ounce of strength in his body, clearing by inches the only obstacle to his freedom.

He was gone in an instant into the night. There was no human awake to witness this magnificent creature do the impossible. But their records reflect that a stallion escaped that night. That's all. Not how. Not his color. Not that they had been after him for so long that they had dedicated three helicopters and untold numbers of men on horseback to his capture.

Only that a stallion had escaped and was not recaptured.

23

RAISON D'ETRE

It was the best of times it was the worst of times.

Weather systems seemed to be running rampant off the west coast, rolling in every few days. Our travel plans were scuttled by five days of snow, wind and rain. I studied the 10-day forecast at weather.com plus everything the California Highway Patrol site had to say. John at the BLM in Reno advised that from now through February or March things would only get worse. There appeared to be a 2-day window between storms the following Friday and Saturday (December 19-20) if the highways at upper elevations were clear. We would have to cross an 8000-foot pass pulling a horse trailer. I told John this was our target and I began to monitor the CHP site several times a day.

The afternoon before we were to leave home the CHP still had two sections of highway closed due to snow from the last storm, but Friday morning they were both clear. One section well to the north was still showing wind warnings, but the forecast from weather.com was 15mph by afternoon, so off we went, sandwiched between two bad weather systems, creating a serious need to have everything work right. Never the best strategy. This would be the longest trip I'd ever driven with a horse trailer. My calculation was twelve and a half hours one way. As we started out I was thankful that trucks don't read elevated adrenaline like horses do.

The trip, mercifully, was relatively uneventful. CHP was still predicting high winds over a twenty mile stretch of highway maybe 100 miles out of Reno but weather.com said no, so we bit our lips and ignored the brightly flashing wind-warning signs and kept going. Weather.com was right.

I had found a hotel with a big open parking lot that could take a horse trailer, a casino unfortunately right in the middle of downtown. We locked up the truck and trailer and ice-skated across the street to a very mediocre dinner but a very warm bed. The next morning we were at it early. The temperature was a frigid 15 degrees, a condition I had never experienced with a diesel truck. At first it wouldn't start at all, which scared me to death. It was only after I pulled out the owner's manual that I realized I was supposed to turn on the key and let the system warm up the engine before starting in cold weather. Who knew? I lived in southern California. Finally it turned over, but the accelerator wasn't working, had no effect at all. And an engine warning light was on... on a Saturday morning! And snow was due in Reno Saturday night.

I let the engine run for almost thirty minutes before the water temperature gauge finally reached into its working range. And at last the accelerator was working. But the engine light was still on. While the engine was warming up I unlocked all the trailer doors... except for one. The key would not turn at all in the lock of the tack room where all the feed and buckets were for the trip home. Kathleen returned to the hotel and called several 24-hours locksmiths, none of whom were answering their phones. She left a cell number. Once the water temperature gauge was in operating range everything seemed to be operating properly so I decided we should drive on out to the BLM, 15 miles north of town. Maybe the engine light would go out as the engine continued to warm up.

It didn't.

On the way out, Kathleen called both of Reno's Dodge dealers. Again, no answers. Just great, I was thinking. We simply could not take off through the mountains with an unhandled pregnant Mustang and an engine warning light on.

When we arrived at the BLM John Parsons and several bright-eyed, eager volunteers were happily awaiting the loading of another Mustang saved.

"Welcome," John said. "Let's get to it."

"Sorry John," I said meekly, "We have a couple of problems we need to deal with before we can load up." I explained the problems. John felt that he could find us a diesel mechanic who could look at the problem with the warning light... and maybe WD40 would take care of the lock. His diesel mechanic was not answering the phone at 7:30 am so he headed out to attack the lock on the trailer tack room. As he strolled past the truck – I've never been able to "stroll" at 15 degrees – he asked casually, "Are you sure your gas cap is screwed down good and tight? Sometimes a loose cap can cause the engine light to come on."

Kathleen whipped open the flap and turned the cap. "Nope," she said. "It was not screwed down to the click."

I raced to the truck cab and turned the key. The engine light was gone. I felt like a ton of bricks had been lifted off my heart.

John then tried WD40 on the lock, but that yielded nothing. He studied it for a moment, and said, "Let me try something." Soon he returned with a small blow torch. He ignited it and aimed it right at the culprit lock. Thirty seconds later we were inside the tack room. I asked him if he could ride back to southern California with us. "What's the temperature down there," he grinned.

The BLM's elaborate system of stalls and aisles with closing and opening gates was set up to make loading very simple. I asked if I could walk down one of the aisles to look in on her before they started. It seemed like a longer walk than it really was. She was standing all alone in a very large stall and looked at me with that quizzical cock of a head that is so often offered up by Cash. I couldn't help but smile.

I'm not sure why this moment had such an impact on me but I shivered a bit as she stared at me, and it wasn't from the cold. We had already agreed on her name. She was, after all, to be my Christmas gift.

"Hello Miss Noelle," I said. "You're coming home with us."

24

CHANGES

The golden stallion's left rear leg had a small cut just above the pastern from scraping the top rail of the barrier as he cleared it. But that was it, and it was a minor cut at that. He had made his way back to where the matriarch had gone down but she was nowhere in sight. That seemed to be a good sign to the stallion. He sniffed the ground until he found the exact place where she had stumbled, then looked off toward the pond where the herd would drink. Even though he needed water he didn't like the idea of spending any more time out in the open than necessary, and he thought the matriarch, if she were able to move a distance, would feel the same. So he moved out at a trot, headed for the trees where they had been surprised by the big machines.

It was farther than he remembered.

The sun was high in the sky by the time he reached his destination. The great stallion scanned the entire horizon and listened intently before entering the stand of trees. He saw her immediately, lying flat on the ground.

The stallion froze in fear.

Then she turned and looked at him, and rolled over onto her stomach. He was about to race over to her when he saw something move, just behind her. A flicker of gold in a small patch of sunlight.

He stepped closer, cautiously, concerned. It was larger than a flicker, wriggling and struggling, slowly lifting itself up onto four very wobbly legs. Apparently for the first time. He had just missed the birth of his brand new filly. And she was the absolute spitting image of the stallion himself.

The matriarch pulled herself to her feet seeming very little the worse for wear from her traumatic experience. She pivoted her hindquarters virtually shoving her bag into the new baby's mouth.

The stallion touched the matriarch's nose and nickered softly.

He had produced many babies with many mares. But never could he remember feeling as happy and as proud of both mother and baby as he felt at that very moment.

The buckskin mare stood in one place all day eating hay out of a big round container, one of many scattered around a large flat area surrounded by tall barriers. This is the way she spent most of her days. There was no movement necessary to eat. And almost none necessary to drink. It had been like this for three months. For nearly two hundred horses. Most of the buckskin's herd stayed close to her and didn't mingle with the strangers. Especially the two-colored filly. Their feet were all overgrown because they were getting no wear. Their muscles were softening because they were getting no movement. And the buckskin's spirit was dissolving away.

It was the same with all the other horses who were penned up with her. Not one seemed to care much about anything. Men would show up in noisy wagons once or twice a day to add hay to the big round containers, and every once in a while one or two horses would be separated from the others and taken away. Add ten, take away two. It had all become routine. Except when horses were added the buckskin and her herd would stir and grow anxious to see if their golden stallion might be among the newcomers. The buckskin would hope so. And hope not.

One day the men who appeared when horses were to be driven out of the pen came in, looked around, and moved slowly toward the buckskin, slapping coils of rope on their legs. She moved away from them but they kept coming. And kept coming. One of them had a long stick like the stick that made her stallion scream. She broke into a trot and circled back into the herd, but they kept coming. Finally she spotted an opening in the barrier that seemed to be her only escape and she galloped through it and down a long row of barriers into another pen. Smaller, empty. There was only one way in or out and it closed behind her.

Soon it was dark. And she saw no horses and no men until once again the sun was rising into the sky and her warm breath was greeting the cold morning with fog.

A man appeared at the opening. Tall, lanky. With no coiled ropes, and no sticks. He took a step closer, his head bowed, his shoulders slumped. And there was no evil in his eyes.

"Hello Miss Noelle," he said. "You're coming home with us."

She blinked.

"We're off on an adventure, you and I. A new journey for both of us. I will love you. And I hope you will love me."

She didn't know what the words meant. They were just noise. But she knew this man was different, and in some small way she understood.

25

LET THEM SUFFER

I am clearly naïve.

Hopelessly wanting to believe that most people will do the right thing. Or at the very least won't go out of their way to do the wrong thing.

My first clue about how silly it is to think like that should've been the number of horses who are still being forced to live in a manner that is diametrically opposed to their genetic needs.

But worse, I suppose, are the numbers of people who not only do not care at all about the few remaining horses in the wild and how they are being treated, they will do whatever they can to get rid of these national treasures without regard for either the law or the lives of the horses.

The documented collusion between ranchers in the western United States and BLM officials, local and not, is staggering. Mind numbing actually. Craig C. Downer, ecologist, life-long wild horse expert, and author of amazing book *The Wild Horse Conspiracy*, was actually threatened by a rancher in an open BLM meeting after speaking in favor of the wild horses and burros being able to live as the law prescribes. The rancher pounded the table, shouted gross obscenities and bellowed, "I'll plaster your brains all over the walls!"

In rural Nevada, wild horses have been shot, poisoned, trapped, and trucked off to slaughter. They have been fenced off from access to their legally rightful water sources and prime feeding and shelter areas. And in 1998 between 800 and 1000 wild horses were shot and killed, many deliberately "gut-shot" so they would wander away from the site of the shooting to die agonizing, prolonged deaths somewhere else, hoping no one would notice. Considerable evidence was amassed and a lengthy trial ensued naming several ranchers but the accused were ultimately let off on a technicality concerning the difficulty of proving conclusively which bullet belonged to which rifle.

I'm sorry to say this but it reminds me of those shameful days when I was coming of age in the south and law enforcement officials, judges, the media, and citizen juries were all colluding in favor of guilty whites and against innocent blacks. That such a thing can actually happen in this country was hard to believe then, and it's just as hard to believe now.

The ranchers accuse wild horses of decimating the land when the horses are outnumbered 150 to 1 by their cattle and sheep who leave behind nothing but bare dirt and cow poop. With the stench of excrement filling the air.

On August 8, 2011, retired BLM wild horse/burro official John Phillips went on the record, on film, expressing his utter disgust for people who blame wild horses and burros for despoiling water holes and western habitats that livestock such as domesticated for-profit cattle and sheep have utterly trashed, not the wild horses!

"Evaluation of Appropriate Management Levels has nothing to do with what's really on the ground," says Phillips. "AML figures from the beginning were influenced by and manipulated for cattlemen. I saw it for myself."

Phillips went on to say the BLM officials are shirking their public trust as they deliberately betray the animals, their public supporters, and the very act and unanimous will of the senators and representatives of the American people.

The following article is reproduced with permission from Las Vegas City Life, written by George Knapp, a Peabody Award-winning investigative reporter for KLAS Channel 8. The article is entitled The BLM Is Not Listening.

Maybe you are one of those hard-bark, Western cowpoke types who doesn't exactly get misty-eyed by the vision of a herd of wild mustangs majestically galloping across the sage-dotted open ranges of Nevada. You think of the mustangs as pests or varmints, an invasive species that needs to be eliminated from public lands so there will be more than enough water and forage for the rightful end-users of the public range — cows.

You remember as a kid when you read all those history books about the vast herds of wild cows that roamed North America in prehistoric times? No? Well, maybe you learned from Western movies about how cows are native to these parts, you know, and about how saber-toothed cows terrorized early settlers and thus had to be domesticated. Clearly, in the eyes of some, millions of cows on the public ranges are not a problem and are not an invasive species, but a few thousand wild horses — which are native to this continent — are destructive, invasive pests that need to go.

No matter what your point of view might be, you have a chance this week to let the government know what you think about its wild horse program. Public meetings are being held to gauge public opinion about horse roundups that almost certainly are planned for a few places in the nearby Spring Mountains, including the idyllic mountain community of Cold Creek, home to a small, beloved herd of mustangs.

Don't get the wrong idea, though. Just because these are public meetings at which the public will be asked for its opinion, you should not assume you will be allowed to actually say anything to the government PR folks who run the get-togethers. They have no intention of standing there and allowing the public to tee off. Typically, the feds and their PR handlers will not allow anyone to stand up and speak. Rather, members of the public are allowed to submit written comments that are carefully and meticulously gathered up, and then — presumably — are promptly shredded for use in recycled toilet paper. They surely play zero role in government decision-making.

Even if you somehow pull off a miracle and manage to tell the BLM that you hate the idea of yet another horse roundup, as hundreds of Nevadans have done over the past several years, it will make not one bit of difference. The decision on when and where and how many horses to capture has already been made, and no amount of opposition to the roundups will matter one tiny bit to BLM or the Forest Service. Their disdain for the public, and especially for wild horse advocates, is palpable.

The other day at a BLM corral near Reno, three BLM wranglers put on a little show of defiance and contempt when they tried to capture a single painted mustang from one of the holding pens. Instead of saddling up their horses to enter the pens where the skittish, recently captured mustangs were baking in the hot sun, these three burly yokels crammed themselves into the front seat of a flatbed truck and then tore into the corral like they were imitating Bo Duke trying to get away from Boss Hogg. Video recorded by a horse advocate shows the rootin'-tootin' cowpokes repeatedly fishtailing their truck and spinning around to take another run at the paint, while scattering every other horse in the pen. They even made a point of coming over to the woman with the camera to taunt her, knowing that the video would make not a whit of difference to their bosses, even if it went viral.

The BLM's virtually unstoppable plan to round up the few wild horses that remain in Southern Nevada comes less than two weeks after the wild horse program was described as abysmal failure in a study conducted for the National Academy of Sciences. The blistering report ripped the BLM a new one, and, in particular, declared the continued program of roundups and long-term storage as counterproductive — for the horses, the range and especially the taxpayers. One likely effect of the constant roundups is that the horses go into survival mode, meaning, they reproduce far in excess of what they might naturally do.

So how did BLM react to such a thorough and embarrassing rebuke of its ongoing policies? A spokesman thanked the NAS for its report, saying the bureau "welcomed it."

(Translation: Go fuck yourself.) And, said an official, the BLM will take the recommendations under advisement. (Translation: You can stick this report far up your scientific ass.) One needs look no further than the plans being evaluated at this week's meetings — plans that call for more roundups of more horses — to understand what the BLM thinks of the NAS scientists and the taxpayers.

BLM will never stop the roundups on its own. Never. The only time it has been thwarted is when citizens have gone to federal court to fight it, and those victories are few and far between. Despite overwhelming public support for the mustang herds, the horses have fared no better in Congress in recent years. Horse advocates don't quite match the political muscle of the cattle industry. Now, more than ever, money talks.

Like I mentioned, maybe you're one of those who don't care about the mustangs, or even one of those who despise them. Nonetheless, you still have a stake in this failed program. The costs have jumped from $20 million a year in 2000 to more than $75 million this year. The main reason is that BLM likes to round up mustangs (based on nonscientific projections about as reliable as a Mystic 8 ball) and then ship them off to private pens owned by friends of BLM managers or former BLM employees, where they languish, out of sight, for the rest of their lives. In light of the fact that there are now more mustangs in captivity than remain on the range, it's no wonder the program is getting so expensive.

There are better ways to do this. The constant pattern of roundups and warehousing simply doesn't work. The NAS study made some suggestions for improvement, but unless BLM is lassoed, hog-tied and forced to change, there is no chance in hell the prevailing anti-mustang sentiment in the bureau will ever do things differently. – *George Knapp*

"Lack of water is a primary excuse given by the BLM for zeroing out herds," John Phillips states in the 2011 filmed interview exposing (criminal) BLM practices. "Yet the water is often present. It's just that the federal officials refuse to assert the wild horses' right to it." He further adamantly insists that the (Free-Roaming Wild Horse and Burro) act of 1971 carries with it *Implied Federal Water Rights* as is the case with other acts establishing wildlife refuges, Indian reservations, etc. and that the BLM and USFS are not upholding viable wild horse and burro populations with entitled water in their legal horse/burro herd areas.

Phillips swears that much of the initial impetus to destroy the program began with the dissemination of pseudo-scientific articles that were shamelessly biased and motivated solely by an animus against the horses and burros in their wild and free state by people who were particularly upset by the wild horses and burros having gained legal status.

And now the BLM is facing a crisis in overload while trying to please their leasing ranchers and wild game hunters. Their holding pens and pastures are full. Adoptions do not come even close to matching the number of horses rounded up, causing the BLM to fracture even more of the laws they're supposed to be enforcing by selling to kill buyers who send the horses off to slaughter plants in Mexico and Canada.

Last weekend, as I write this, the Federal government fell to a new low assisting an auction in Fallon, Nevada, reported in Esquire Magazine by Andrew Cohen: "Babies of weaning age -- maybe three months old -- were pulled from their mothers and immediately herded into the auction ring, one by one, crying and looking for their mothers as they were sold to the highest (kill buyer) bidder. Then their mothers followed, pushed into the ring in groups of 5-6 horses, huddled together, terrified and auctioned in lots and purchased by a kill buyer. It was brutal."

The investigative journalism site Pro Publica reports that BLM officials state that they screen buyers of horses they have rounded up and they are adamant that no wild horses ever go to slaughter. Yet, a little-known Colorado livestock hauler named Tom Davis has purchased at least 1700 wild horses for $10 a head in less than three years according to BLM sales records.

Like all buyers, Davis signs contracts promising that animals bought from the program will not be slaughtered and insists he finds them good homes. But Davis is a long-time advocate of horse slaughter. By his own account, he has ducked Colorado law to move animals across state lines and will not say where they end up. He continues to buy wild horses for slaughter from Indian reservations, which are not protected by the same laws. And since 2010, he has been seeking investors for a slaughterhouse of his own.

Some BLM employees say privately that wild horse program officials may not want to look too closely at Davis. The agency has more wild horses than it knows what to do with, they say, and Davis has become a relief valve for a federal program plagued by conflict and cost over-runs.

"They are under a lot of pressure in Washington to make numbers," said a BLM corral manager who did not want his name used because he feared retribution from the agency's national office. "Maybe that is what this is about. They probably don't want to look too careful at this guy."

Davis said in an interview with Pro Publica that BLM employees occasionally asked where his horses ended up, but said he tells them it's "none of your damn business."

"They never question me too hard. It makes 'em look good if they're movin' these horses, see?" he said. "Every horse I take from them saves them a lot of money. I'm doing them a favor. I'm doing the American people a favor."

Asked if he would provide records of his sales, he responded, "Ain't no way in hell."

Brand documents leave almost 1,000 of Davis's wild horses unaccounted for. That means, according to Colorado law, they should still be within 75 miles of his residence -- if he has complied with the law.

Asked if this was the case, Davis first said the horses were still on 160 acres of land he leases from the state of Colorado. Then he said some had been shipped out of state without brand inspections, a misdemeanor punishable by up to 18 months in jail and a $1,000 fine.

"Since when is anything in this country done legal?" Davis said in a phone interview.

Davis, by the way, lives in a little valley in Colorado just down the road from Ken Salazar, the immediate past Secretary of the Interior who managed the BLM and who has hired Davis often to haul cattle for him.

Coincidence?

Not even remotely likely.

Where does all this end?

Unfortunately with us. All of us.

As George Knapp said in his article (above), "Unless BLM is lassoed, hog-tied and forced to change, there is no chance in hell the prevailing anti-mustang sentiment in the bureau will ever do things differently. "

And the only way to lasso, hog-tie, and force the BLM to change is with the law. The courts. And to do that, lawyers are needed who can donate time to lawsuits against the BLM. If you're a lawyer, please consider this. I believe it's the only ultimate way to save what's left of the horses in the wild. The only way to finally bring the BLM to its knees. If you're just a lover of horses or a concerned citizen and know some lawyers, please tell them about it. And maybe donate some money to help pay for lawyers who cannot afford to donate their time. The ultimate solution, in my humble opinion, lies there. In hammering the BLM in the courts with facts and law so hard and so often that they lose enough to be forced by the courts to buy back cattle grazing rights on public lands that were designated for the horses in the 1971 Law. And to return the horses to those lands they were granted. And to allow the cougars, bears, and wolves and other wildlife to restructure the natural ecological balance required by the law.

It's a long and winding road, but it can happen.

It should happen.

26

GROWN UP

The golden stallion's baby had grown into a beautiful young filly, golden like her father, with the very same tiny white speckle hiding under her forelock. The stallion was very proud. She was now three years old and had been courted by suitors for more than a year. But none of them had measured up to her doting daddy's standards.

His new herd had grown as well with two new mares he had captured from other stallions. One had birthed a colt of his who was nearing two years old and the other had come to the herd pregnant by her previous stallion and had given birth to a feisty young sorrel colt now between two and three years old. This colt would probably not be allowed to stay in the herd much longer and would have to join a local bachelor band until he became old enough to capture some mares of his own. The matriarch still ruled the little herd and had a new filly barely three months old. She wore her mother's color, a dark bay.

So far none of the new babies had been introduced to the terror of the big thundering machines chasing them. The stallion and the matriarch had seen them in the distance on occasion but none had come after them recently, and that made him happy.

But not comfortable.

He still felt uneasy about the way things were. And the future. He felt that way every day.

The golden filly had learned a lot from the stallion and the matriarch. And she was definitely the boss of the younger set in the herd, even the rambunctious colt to whom she was not related. Although it was clear to all that she liked him.

Most of the time she stayed close to her papa but on this day she and the other two youngsters were off down the slope cavorting, chasing each other, and burning off energy. The stallion, his mares, and the new baby watched from the trees. Over the last few years the stallion and the matriarch had begun a pattern of staying in or near good cover, like a stand of trees, when the sun was up and travelling only at night. The machines were never out at night. But it was often difficult to keep the energy of the young ones all locked up during the day. This day was no exception.

At one point the stallion whinnied at them.

Too far! Come back this way!

And they did. A little.

The stallion whinnied again.

Not enough! Come on!

But the filly was running circles and kicking her heels up and didn't hear him. Or pretended she didn't. She was good at that.

The stallion snorted, and turned away to check on the matriarch and her young foal. The baby was nursing and the matriarch was dozing. Or appeared to be until she swung around and nipped at the foal. *Watch those new teeth please!*

The sound was sudden and spun the stallion around. The pounding thumping roar that was all too familiar. And there it was. The machine, dropping out of the sky. Dropping... dropping! Right down onto his three babies. He threw his head toward the heavens and bellowed as if his own life were being ripped away.

And in so many ways it was.

27

NOW IT'S PERSONAL

Above is an un-retouched photograph by Laura Leigh of our Miss Saffron (far right) and two young herd mates on the day they were brutally chased and rounded up by a BLM helicopter whose skids were barely ten feet off of her back.

Saffron was just over three months pregnant on this day. Neither the BLM, nor, presumably, her papa have any knowledge of who the daddy might have been. But Kathleen and I believe he's in this photo.

We thank Laura Leigh so much because the photo brings home to us more than just about anything else could how calloused and arrogant and without a soul these people are. When we discovered that Laura had been there, at the right place on the right date, shooting photos and videos, we sent her photos of Saffy and she sent back several for us to examine. We aren't sure about a couple of the others, but about the above photo we are very certain. When it is enlarged there are several markings and patterns that show clearly. Saffron always runs with her tail straight out. She has a very short off-white sock just barely above her left rear pastern. Her mane falls on her right side except for a very small portion just above her withers, which falls to the left. She has a dark gray-black muzzle all the way around, a very definitive head shape, and the tiniest white spot under her forelock with no other facial markings. And in this photo she definitely looks like... well, herself.

After they were forced to run for a very long time, finally into a small holding pen, the mares were separated from the stallions and colts. After a period of being held in Nevada, Miss Saffron was shipped to a BLM facility in southern California and ultimately to another BLM holding facility in Piney Woods, Mississippi. Twice she was shipped out to local adoption events, one in Kentucky and one in Florida. Neither time was she adopted.

If any horse is passed over for adoption three times the BLM can then make an immediate outright "sale" of that horse for as little as $10. With normal adoptions the cost is $125 and the BLM retains the ownership title to that horse for one year, then follows up to assess whether the horse is being cared for properly before passing along ownership title. But with an outright sale the title passes immediately, and it has been documented that many if not most of those sales wind up going to kill buyers who transport the horses to slaughter houses in Mexico and Canada.

If there is a rational reason why a horse's life is suddenly devalued to basically zero because she has been passed over an arbitrary number of times I would love to hear it. This is some warped rationalization tangled up in a view that this life is worth spending thousands and thousands of dollars to save... unless she doesn't get adopted right now. Then it's worth nothing.

When we met Miss Saffron on March 17th, 2012, she had only one strike left before she and her unborn baby would've been gone. Her third adoption event was scheduled for the afternoon of the same morning we met and adopted this most incredible trusting soul.

Makes me shiver.

And makes me wonder. How in the world, after all she had been through, could she meet us with such willingness? Give us the benefit of the doubt? Label us as innocent until proven guilty? And trust herself to open the door to trust?

There was little question about her previous experiences with humans. She had just been rounded up, ripped away from her family, and moved across the country four times by an agency of the federal government who has proven repeatedly how little they care about wild horses.

So our plan was to ensure that from first sight we were not equated with the enemy. Everything we did was from the perspective that whatever her problems might have been in the past, none of them were her fault. And they could all be fixed by proving to her that we were different from anything she had ever experienced. That we were not "that way". Whatever "that way" happened to be. Which, of course, we didn't know. So that meant we had to exclude *every*thing.

Which is why we spent 35 days doing absolutely nothing with Miss Saffron except to feed her, and be available. And, for 32 of those days, be sweet and loving to her new baby.

Without any knowledge of the learning experience we were to have in the next chapter we were trying to wipe her slate clean. To give her a fresh start. As if she had never before seen a human being. And then wait for her to choose, of her own free will, to trust us.

We now know why it worked.

28

A BLANK SLATE

Have you ever wondered what it would be like to meet a horse who had never seen a human before?

Never been roped and jerked and pulled around by one. Never been physically forced to do things it didn't want to do. Or was afraid to do. Never been frightened out of its wits by a helicopter trying to run over it. Or chased by screeching men on other horses. Or poked, kicked, and whipped. Or electric shocked into submission.

Kelly Marks wondered.

And she set out to find such a horse.

She believed that horses would much rather be in relationship than not, even with a predator were that possible. Why? Because the horse's number one concern in life is safety. Security. A good relationship means the horse feels safe and secure. It means the horse can trust. And will not be living in fear.

Kelly had a theory that every behavior problem she had ever witnessed in her training demonstrations was caused somehow, at some point in time, by a human. Perhaps inadvertently. Perhaps not. Perhaps years and years ago. But caused by a human.

So she wanted to find a group of wild horses somewhere on the planet that had never encountered a human. Never been near one. Preferably never even seen one. And then she wanted to start one of those horses. To Join Up and ride one of those horses. To approach them so softly, so carefully, that no signal would ever be sent that could possibly be interpreted as something for the horse to be fearful about.

What, she wondered, would happen?

Starting with a completely blank slate, no past history and no embedded fears of humans, could she convince such a horse that he had nothing to fear from her. Or would fear even be a factor so long as she did nothing that would encourage fear.

She knew from her work with hundreds and hundreds of horses that when a horse is afraid of a particular human the fear can often translate to all humans. Guilty until proven innocent. Which creates barriers that must be overcome on the road to relationship.

Her theory: if she could find horses who had never ever encountered a human then the horse should have no baggage. No pre-conceived fear. As long as Kelly did nothing that would cause the horse to see her as predatory, she should be considered nothing more potentially harmful than a rabbit. Or a squirrel. Or a deer. If she could prove this truth it could be immensely helpful when working with domesticated horses, and when teaching newcomers or people working with new horses what to expect and how very careful they need to be to not frighten this prey animal.

Kelly Marks is the founder of Intelligent Horsemanship in the UK and is a Monty Roberts Scholar and a Lifetime Protégée. And she has become Monty's right hand in the UK and Europe. But she wanted to do this on her own and Monty was against it. He felt it was too dangerous.

But she found a herd in Namibia in southwest Africa that had never encountered humans in any way. Many, if not most, had never even seen a human. She and two others on her team recruited some locals and a documentary film crew and off they went.

Even Kelly was surprised at the result.

One of Kelly's team is her rider, Grant Bazin. In her demonstrations she rarely does the first ride on a horse herself. Among other reasons it would be very difficult for her to concentrate on her safety while speaking continuously to an audience. So her very experienced rider goes with her whenever work is at hand. The third member of the team is a very knowledgeable and experienced equine behaviorist, Ian Vandenberghe. Because Kelly's number one job is to cause the horse to feel safe, comfortable with her, she believes that looking the horse directly in the eye could give the horse reason to believe she is a predator. So it is her behaviorist's job is to pick up information from the horse's eyes and body language that Kelly might not see and relay that information to Kelly.

The first thing they did was encircle the watering facility in the south African desert with posts, then made walls out of lightweight sack material. They had their eye on selecting a horse from a bachelor band so as to not disrupt an existing family band, which they accomplished without incident. The isolated stallion was named Muddy Waters because he liked to splash water onto the parched earth and then roll in it. Once Muddy was isolated Kelly immediately poured buckets of water onto the ground and then sat in a chair nearby and talked to him as he sniffed out the puddle and then rolled in it.

This fair lassie could be alright he was probably thinking.

Their entire procedure is immortalized in a documentary available for viewing online. The link is at the end of this chapter. But suffice to say it went so smoothly that Kelly decided to be the first to ride this horse who heretofore had never even seen a human much less had any close encounters with one. She did everything absolutely right and I never once saw even the slightest indication of resistance or fear. In fact, it went so smoothly that they thought it might be a fluke, so they selected another stallion from the bachelor group to go through the same process, only this time Grant would be first up.

And, again, everything went without a hitch. It's amazing to see them scratching and rubbing these horses everywhere possible. Including their ears! With no negative reaction at all. And riding them together as if they had all been a team forever.

Two wild horses who had never been subjected to harrowing helicopter roundups and rough treatment from wranglers. Had never been trained by harsh or cruel means. Had never been exposed to humans who say, "You will do what I tell you or else!"

Which tells me that every behavior problem expressed by a horse, anywhere, everywhere, originates in an experience with a human.

And it tells me how very, very careful, and quiet, and calm, and comforting one needs to be when beginning with any horse. It also tells me, when added to our experience with Saffron, that a horse who has had experiences with humans can start anew. Can be taken back to the beginning. The slate can be wiped clean. It might take longer to eliminate a history than to begin with a horse who has never known humans, but once done, it's quite like starting fresh. Once Saffron made the choice to discard her previous experiences and trust us, as mentioned before, it was as if she had thrown a switch. She was not just "in", she was *all* in. Just like the two wild horses in Namibia.

Another awesome aspect of the African experience is that both of these horses were not just *wild*, they were *stallions*. Almost everyone I've ever asked about stallions says, in one form or another, "Oh, stallions are scary. Too much testosterone! Gotta be really careful around them. They'll kill you in a heartbeat. Don't even try it."

Not to say that you shouldn't be careful around domestic stallions. I suspect that reactions to bad human experiences with mares and geldings could be doubled or tripled if a stallion has been abused.

But the few I've been around, who were brought up and trained with care and compassion, have been as delightful as any other horse anywhere.

The entire Namibian experience was only six days and the building of the pens took the first day and a half. The most amazing thing happened on the sixth day when Kelly and Grant rode these two horses out of the pens – bareback! - to turn them back into the wild. I won't ruin it for you… but do watch the documentary all the way to the end. You will save the link forever. Which is:

http://vimeo.com/33062665

Those two horses were living the life *they* wanted to live. They were happy.

They had no reason to believe they should be afraid of the humans they encountered. And that belief was reinforced by the humans.

So long as Kelly and her team never once did anything that even approached causing the horses to be afraid, they were never afraid. Never reactive. They were using the thinking side of their brain at all times. *How can I help? How do I figure this out?*

And that is simply the best lesson ever!

29

SYNTHESIS

The soul of this horse was born wild. To deny that birth-right is to diminish her soul, and her spirit. To deny that genetic reality is to ensure stress throughout this horse's life that will diminish longevity, health, and happiness.

Why would we do that? To any horse? Why would we be that cruel?

This horse will never be forced to live in a stall. Nor should any so-called domestic horse or any horses living in the wild. The genetics of all horses have been designed over millions of years to live outside 24/7. To graze, from the ground. To get lots and lots of movement while grazing. To be able to see predators coming. And to be with other horses for safety. Being locked in a stall, away from all that, causes emotional and physical stress, which in turn results in all sorts of health problems and stall vices.

Wild horses don't eat sugar. Like molasses. Or anything that turns to sugar when entering the body, like oats, or corn, or virtually any other grain. A horse's Non Structured Carbohydrate level (sugar) should never be above 10%. To be so is to risk insulin resistance, laminitis, and other health problems.

Wild horses never eat 100% alfalfa, which is a legume, not grass. Grass is 90% of a horse's diet living in the wild. Grass or grass hay should be accessible free choice around the clock.

The bottom line is that whenever there is a question about lifestyle, diet, feet, behavior, or just about anything else related to the horse, the answer can be found in the answer to this question. *What would the horse be doing for himself if he were living in the wild of the American west.* Because every horse on the planet was born wild. And, genetically speaking, still is.

By no means does any of this imply a life without humans. The horse loves to be in relationship. Prefers it. Even with us humans if the relationship is approached with understanding, respect, and compassion. Kelly Marks proved that, once and for all, with her trip to Namibia. And she identified the perfect place from which to approach that relationship. Before the horse has ever experienced any human. Not an easy horse to find.

But, as we discovered with Saffron, negative marks on a slate from previous humans can be erased. Wiped clean. It just takes time. We allowed Saffron to take the time that she needed to clean her own slate and when she was done, like the wild horses in Namibia, she was able to experience trust without fear.

When we discovered that everything begins and ends with the wild horse, we had to reorient ourselves. Not just for the horse living in the wild but for *every* horse on the planet. Because far too many of both are living under downright shameful conditions.

Horses living in the wilds of the American west are being harassed and hounded by our own federal government who is reducing their numbers at an alarming rate and allowing the shipment many off to slaughter plants. Others are stripped of their families and their lifestyle in the wild and forced into traditional domestic captivity.

Stalls.

We have eight horses: a rescued American Saddlebred, three mustangs straight out of the wild, two Arabians, a paint and a quarter horse. They live out 24/7. Together as a herd. They have free-choice access to pasture or grass hay. They have access to the barn breezeway, at their choice, but they have no stalls. And we have no colic, no laminitis, no strangles, no insulin resistance, no ulcers, no founder, no navicular issues, no cribbing, pawing, kicking, weaving, pacing, or biting. We have happy, healthy horses, each of whom come when they're called, and each of whom will walk with me at liberty wherever I would like them to go (*most* of the time).

Our mission, and that of this book, is to inspire that lifestyle for every horse on the planet, because none of them can speak for themselves. They have no choice or voice in these matters. No vote.

The opening dedication of this book reads:

For every horse alive today and all of those to come... and for every human who has never experienced the wonder of being close to at least one of them.

Because when you have experienced the very soul of a horse you will be changed. You cannot help but fall in love. And love drives everything else. A popular movie once put it: *Love means never having to say you're sorry.*

To the horses.

Or yourself.

Love drives caring. And caring drives action. And today's horses need action.

Those in domestic care, most of them, need a complete makeover, a lifestyle change replicating what their genetics need.

Those in the wild and those pulled from the wild and held in ghetto-like pens need to be returned to the lands that are legally theirs, to live in a natural ecological environment as the law prescribes... and to otherwise be left alone!

Preservation of the horses in the wild is not only their birthright, it is their legal right, and they provide a valuable model of lifestyle for every horse living in domestic care.

When I gave Cash the choice of choice and he chose me, he left me with no alternative. No longer could it be what I wanted, but rather what he needed. And what he needed, it turned out, is what his fifty-two million years of genetics demanded for his long, healthy, and happy life. A lifestyle as close to what his kindred in the wild are living as we could possibly make it.

Discovering the mysteries of the horse has been a never-ending journey, but the rewards are an elixir. The soul prospers from sharing, caring, relating, and fulfilling. Nothing can make you feel better than doing something good for another being. Not cars. Not houses. Not facelifts. Not blue ribbons or trophies. And there is nothing more important in life than love. Not money. Not status. Not winning.

Try it and you will understand what I mean. Apply it to the horses, and your life. It is the synthesis of this book and why it came into being.

May it be a crack in the armor, a small breeze if not the strong winds of change, a resource for what needs to be done. A celebration of the fact that every horse on the planet is born wild.

And should be allowed to live that way.

Follow Joe & Kathleen's Journey

From no horses and no clue to stumbling through mistakes, fear, fascination and frustration on a collision course with the ultimate discovery that something was very wrong in the world of horses.

Read the National Best Seller
The Soul of a Horse
Life Lessons from the Herd

…and the new…

Horses & Stress
*Eliminating the Root Cause of
Most Health, Hoof, and Behavior Problems*

http://thesoulofahorse.com

http://thesoulofahores.com/blog

All of the links in this book are live links in the eBook editions available at Amazon Kindle, Barnes & Noble Nook, and Apple iBooks, and all photos are in color.

About the Author

In His Words

One evening, way back, at the wrap party for the crew of the original Benji, I was trying to convince our continuity supervisor that I wasn't *of* Hollywood, either geographically or spiritually. She stopped me cold in mid-sentence, her hand in the air, and said, "What you do speaks so loudly I cannot hear what you say."

I've never forgotten it.

What you do speaks so loudly I cannot hear what you say.

To me that means do it first, then there's little need to *say* anything.

That phrase, and the forty years that followed its utterance, have worked together to craft who I am. What I do. Which I hope has managed to come before what I say, at least most of the time.

Yet, here I am at the end of another book. Another vehicle for words. And words, undeniably, are the building blocks of what I say. But I hope that the words in this book have melted into folds of what is being done, not what is being said, for that is their purpose here. To create the experience for you that you might live it with us, *do* it with us. *Feel* it with us. Ignoring the words themselves.

In that spirit, I also hope you might ignore that you have possibly read some of the words that follow at the end of the original *The Soul of a Horse,* because I believe they so validly describe who I am and what I do that I can find no rational reason to use them any differently.

It is something of a miracle that we are where we are today. If the last Benji movie, *Benji Off the Leash,* had been a big success, we would've never owned horses, and *The Soul of a Horse* along with nine other books chronicling our journey and mission with horses would've never been written. And thousands of horses across the planet would not be leading happier healthier lives. The movie was not a big success. It was unable to compete as an independent film against the huge promotional dollars being spent by the Hollywood studios these days. That experience left a huge, gaping hole in my life. I was convinced that *Benji Off the Leash* was going to raise the bar for family films. Be an example that would show Hollywood the error of its ways. It had a strong story that set a good example, without the use of four-letter words, sexual innuendos, or violence. I was certain that God was using *Benji Off the Leash* to prove once and for all that good stories do not need to lower the bar to entertain. It was clear, at least to me, that God had been involved in the movie from the beginning, that He wanted it to be made. The money was raised in record time. We were forced to accept Utah as a production location, against our wishes, but once we were there, many of the usual production problems miraculously vanished. And we found Tony DiLorenzo, a young composer searching for his first movie. He wrote an amazing score that we could never have afforded with a seasoned composer, and I believe Tony will become one of the finest film composers in the business.

Yet with all of that, the film did not do well.

And there was this huge hole to fill.

When depression tries to claw its ugly self into your being, there are but two choices. Give in to it, or grab it by its scrawny neck, sling it to the ground, and pull yourself out of that hole.

Growth always seems to arise out of adversity.

I, of course, didn't know it when it was happening, but God was telling me it was time to move on. Another need. Another place to make a difference.

If the movie had been even marginally successful, He knew I'd be off working on another one.

But I wasn't to go there.

God recruited Kathleen to do the dirty work. To lead me unwittingly down this new path until, quite unexpectedly, an amazing journey of discovery spread out before us.

A new passion was born.

We were on a collision course with the fact that something was very wrong in the world of horses. And there had to be a way to make it better.

So I must thank God for never failing to do whatever it takes to make me listen, no matter how hard I try not to. For the tough love I so often need. For caring that much. And for using me as a humbled instrument of His will.

And I thank the investors in *Benji Off the Leash*, dear friends all. At best it will be a long time until you recoup your investment, yet I have never lost your support, or your friendship. In addition to funding a terrific movie with a wonderful message, you have inadvertently made a huge difference for horses everywhere.

During the promotion of the film, one of the publicists set up a radio interview by telephone with Dr. Marty Becker, well-known author, syndicated columnist, radio host, and *Good Morning America's* vet in residence. A week or so after the interview Marty called and asked if it would be possible for me to bring Benji to a fund-raiser in his hometown of Bonners Ferry, Idaho. We were in the middle of a coast-to-coast, major market promotional tour for the film and he was asking that we pause for two days and come to a town of 2,700 people for a benefit screening. "We could also do one in the neighboring town of Sandpoint," he added. A much bigger town, almost 8,000 people.

It was clearly another God thing, because I took one look at Marty and Teresa's beautiful ranch – and their horses – and convinced everyone involved that it would be a nice breather between Seattle and Chicago. Kathleen met me in Spokane and we drove up to Bonners Ferry for a perfectly wonderful two days nurturing a pair of new lifelong friendships.

Why does any of that matter? Because if it hadn't been for the movie, the investors, and God, this most unusual meeting with Marty Becker would have never happened. And if the meeting had never happened, Marty Becker would never have become such a giving and loving friend, and he would've never introduced me to his literary agent, David Vigliano, easily one of the best in all the world. If I had never met David, it stands to reason that he never would have become my agent and I suspect that none of this would've ever happened. Certainly, without David, *The Soul of a Horse* would've never made it to Shaye Areheart, the most loving publisher on the planet.

So from the bottom of my heart, thank you so much, Dr. Marty Becker. Maybe our horses will be pasture mates someday. And thank you David Vigliano for loving the book right from the get go. For believing. And for saying exactly the right thing every time I needed it. Thank you Shaye Areheart for having the faith to put the power of America's largest publishing house behind my meager words. And turning it into a National Best Seller, my first time out. I'm still aghast.

Thank you, Monty Roberts, for your friendship and for being there with Join-Up as we began this process. If we hadn't given our horses that choice to be with us, right in the beginning, our entire experience would have been sadly different, for it was that moment of Join-Up with Cash that caused me to change from owner to brother. From *like* to *love*. From the boss to a member of the herd, and a true leader. You have blessed me with the soul of a horse.

I thank all the clinicians, trimmers, vets, and authors listed in the Resources section of this book, many of whom have become friends since those early days not really so long ago. Thank you for sharing your decades and decades of rich experience that allowed us to get so quickly up to speed, to understand the truth, and to become yet another messenger to carry your mission forward.

Thank you, Cash, Noelle, Saffy, Stormy, and all of our horses. Each of you has such a wonderfully unique personality, and you have brought so much into our lives. But especially, Cash, I wonder if you understand how very much you mean to me. When you cock your head and peer straight into my soul, I believe, somehow, that you do.

Lastly, there is my chief editor, the love of my life and my second soul mate, Kathleen. How does one become so fortunate as to have two such intelligent, caring, compassionate soul mates in one lifetime? Whenever I'm buried in a project, Kathleen is always there. If I'm editing a film, she consults every evening on what we've edited that day. And she's so brutally honest that afterward we might not speak for hours. It's difficult, emotional work that deserves combat pay. The same is true with this book. She read every word, every chapter, over and over again.

"I don't see any changes," she might say.

"What do you mean? The third word in the eighteenth paragraph is changed."

Combat pay indeed.

Thank you so much, Sweetie, not only for your help and support, your love, your glorious ideas, and, yes, for the titles of many of the books, the ones with good titles. But also for allowing me to tell your side of this journey as it actually was and is: fearful, frustrating, embarrassing, and finally confident. I'm sure there have been times when you simply wanted to quit and walk away. This, as all the others, is your book as much as mine. I love you so much.

MORE ABOUT THE AUTHOR

Joe is the creator of the canine superstar Benji and the writer, producer, and director of all five Benji theatrical films and various television programs. He has authored eighteen books including three novelizations of his own screenplays, eleven horse-related books, and a book about his relationship with God. Joe spends time speaking around the country on behalf of kids, homeless pets, wild horses, and proper care for all horses. He has two sons, Joe Camp III and Brandon Camp, both movers and shakers in the movie business, and three step children in college. He and his wife Kathleen, eight horses, six chickens, five dogs, and a cat live in rural middle Tennessee. For more about Joe visit thesoulofahorse.com.

RESOURCES

No Agenda Time

We sometimes call it *Join Up Without a Round Pen*. No-Agenda Time is a ritual Kathleen and I began with Noelle after Malachi died. The goal at the time was to just give her a bit of unstressed compassion and companionship. We'd go into Malachi's playpen, open it up to Noelle, scatter a bit of hay around our feet, then sit there and talk, with no agenda whatsoever. Seriously, none. It yielded some of the best moments and lessons ever with Noelle. It took a bit of post analysis to realize what was going on during those times. And when we did we decided that we should use No Agenda Time with Saffron when we first adopted her.

Every evening we would sit in the paddock where Saffron and Stormy ate their dinner and talk about our day, with no agenda related to the horses. We totally and completely ignored Saffron. Stormy was already bonded, probably since her first day. But with Saffron the purpose was to attempt nothing whatsoever with her until she decided of her own free choice, her own free will, that she trusted us and would like to have a relationship with us. Up until this point I had not been able to touch her at all. Anywhere. And I could not stand up with her anywhere close or she'd be gone.

There was obviously some level of trust working because she never once got upset with my imprinting of her new baby. I could touch, hold, and rub her. But not her mom.

One evening Stormy fell asleep right at Kathleen's feet. Actually *on* her feet. Shortly after, her mom, Miss Saffron, an untouched mustang from the wild just a few weeks earlier, turned away and sauntered off to the water tub for a drink, maybe fifty feet away. Leaving her baby asleep on Kathleen's boot. She wouldn't even let Stormy interact with the other horses through the fence. And had never before left her in our care. The trust it took to do that both surprised and overwhelmed us. And that was surely a signal. Five days later, on the evening of my birthday, Saffy gave me the best gift I could've asked for. Her ever so slowly eroding trust barrier suddenly cracked, crumbled, and fell completely away.

With no advance notice she was suddenly all over me. Blowing noses, rubbing my cheek. Accepting scratches and rubs everywhere I could never touch before. Her neck, under her jaw, down her shoulder and leg. Her rib cage. Behind her ear. See the post <u>An Amazing Birthday Gift from a Wild Mustang</u>

You might remember that, for me, the most important element in Monty Roberts' Join Up is that the choice to join up belongs to the horse. It is not forced by the human. And when the horse makes that choice freely, of its own free will, everything changes. No-Agenda time takes longer than Monty's Join Up (which usually works for him in 30 to 40 minutes). This experiment with Saffron took 35 days, but when it happened everything changed right before our eyes. Everything! As if she had just thrown a light switch.

Happy Birthday she said!

I know friends who have accomplished this type of Join Up by just sitting alone in the middle of a pen, perhaps reading a book. Or working on something. Maybe studying.

I personally prefer it with two people. With two people, engrossed in conversation with each other it adds an element of exclusion which seems to emphasize that there is no agenda relative to the horse. The horse can do whatever the horse wants to. We generally have some hay scattered near our feet, just to force closeness, which, again, when ignored seems to emphasize no agenda. It will probably take weeks. Four weeks is a pretty good average of time from our experience and from others I've spoken with.

But you must wait for the horse to tell you that she accepts you, trusts you, and would like to be in relationship. That usually comes in the form of the horse touching you, maybe on your shoulder, or the side of your face. Perhaps blowing in your ear. Or just resting her chin on your shoulder and taking a nap. And allowing you to do things she would have not allowed ten minutes before. Rubbing, touching, scratching. Wherever. But especially often freaky areas, like ears, feet, belly, places like that.

But you must resist the temptation to do anything at all until the horse has taken that first step. That's when everything changes. If you try to reach out, touch, get her to sniff you, or sneak a little rub, the response will always be conditional. And if she responds with fright you could well be setting yourself back a lot. When you do nothing until she makes her choice, the response will be total, *all in*.

Saffron sniffed my jeans a couple of times and even my gloves once, but even though those moments were enticing, I knew they were *not* commitments. They were merely exploratory musings. So do not jump in early.

How do you know which method to use? A traditional Join Up? Pat Parelli's method? Or No Agenda Time? I would say if you *know* that the horse has had some bad experiences with humans who came before you, I would use No Agenda Time. If you *know* the horse has had good experiences with previous humans and is familiar with halters, maybe even has been ridden, perhaps try the traditional Join Up. With any mustang – my opinion only – I would use No Agenda Time just to be safe. Had we known when Noelle came to us what we know today, and had we used No Agenda Time back then, I believe we would have a very different relationship with her today.

Try it. But let the horse make the choices. Don't be an opportunist. Let it roll along like a family conversation and ultimately the horse will begin to feel very safe and trusting, and one day that switch will flick on and everything will be different. In an instant. And how terrific that feels.

As I write this, we are back at it with Noelle. Take two. We will report.

Chronology of the Horse's Evolution

Most of the following can be found at the American Academy for the Advancement of Science (AAAS). Or merely Google "Evolution of the Horse". All of your "hits" won't be scientific, but most will be. And see Craig Downer's book *The Wild Horse Conspiracy*, Chapter One, available on Amazon in print and Kindle versions.

Remains of the earliest animal anywhere in the world to bear recognizably horse-like anatomy were found in the Idaho/Utah/Wyoming area dating 52 million years ago.

Three-and-a-half million years ago the now famous fossils found near Hageman, Idaho represent the oldest remains of the fully evolved genus Equus, roughly the size and weight of today's Arabian horse. At this time the horse had not yet migrated across the Bering Strait Land Bridge and spread throughout the world.

Carbon-14 datings of mitochondrial DNA by Dr. Ann Forsten have substantiated the origin of the modern horse in North America at 1.7 million years ago.

Bones found in South America from horses that had migrated from North America dated one million years ago appear indistinguishable from Equus caballus (the modern day domestic horse).

DNA sequences taken from long bone remains of horses found preserved in the Alaskan permafrost deposits dated 12,000 to 28,000 years ago differ by as little as 1.2% from the horse in your back yard.

When the Spanish brought the horse to America they were bringing him home. Back to his native land. Wearing the same genetics, the same DNA sequencing he was wearing when he left, and when those left behind were wiped out, if in fact they were, by some unknown cataclysm 2000 to 10,000 years ago. Whether or not the horse was actually wiped out is now under scientific scrutiny because of recent archeological discoveries.

Either way, the wild horse is as native and indigenous to North America as the Bengal tiger is to India or the lion is to Africa and it is of no significance whether he was missing for a short number of years because the horse had already migrated across the Bering Strait Land Bridge and spread into the rest of the world.

Which, at the very least, makes him what is termed *re-introduced native wildlife*.

The horse, therefore, by definition, is indigenous. And native. Much to the frustration of the BLM, the cattle ranchers, and the big game hunters.

Wild Horse Links, Advocates, Videos

The Cloud Foundation
http://www.thecloudfoundation.org/

Ginger Kathren's non- profit Cloud Foundation is dedicated to preventing the extinction of Cloud's herd through education, media events and programming, and public involvement. The Foundation is also determined to protect other wild horse herds on public lands, especially isolated herds with unique characteristics and historical significance.

"I began to realize that we were losing America's wild horses," Ginger says. "They are rounded up by the thousand, losing in an instant what they value most--freedom and family. I realized that even Cloud and his family were in danger."

Cloud is a pale palomino wild stallion living in the Pryor Mountains on the Montana/Wyoming border. His life has been documented from the day of his birth by Emmy-winning filmmaker & TCF's Executive Director Ginger Kathrens. Her films about Cloud, "Cloud: Wild Stallions of the Rockies," "Cloud's Legacy: The Wild Stallion Returns," and the latest film "Cloud: Challenge of the Stallions" all aired on PBS' Nature series and represent the only continuous documentation of a wild animal from birth in our hemisphere. Cloud is now eighteen, born May 29, 1995, and the last film (Cloud: Challenge of the Stallions) is the absolute best film about wild horses I ever hope to see.

Go here to read more, watch videos, and buy the PBS Cloud DVDs. Every dollar goes to The Cloud Foundation: http://www.thecloudfoundation.org/

Wild Horse Education
http://wildhorseeducation.org/

"In 1971 something truly remarkable happened. In response to public pressure, both houses of Congress unanimously passed a bill. Congress' intent clearly was to protect and preserve America's free-roaming horse herds and proscribe methods by which the Secretaries of Interior and Agriculture were to manage those herds.

"But somewhere in the implementation of the Act, something went terribly wrong. In its findings, Congress declared, "these horses and burros are fast disappearing from the American scene." However the agency tasked by Congress to protect and preserve these horses became a machine that removed more horses from public lands than any other entity in modern history."

Laura Leigh's non-profit Wild Horse Education attends roundups, files and attends to lawsuits against the BLM and the USFS, does investigative work, and develops, prints, and distributes information, facts, and statistics to educate wild horse advocates and adversaries. She's a non-stop machine and needs your help. Go here to read more and watch videos that Laura has filmed at actual roundups. http://wildhorseeducation.org/

American Wild Horse Preservation
http://wildhorsepreservation.org/

The American Wild Horse Preservation Campaign (AWHPC) is dedicated to preserving American wild horses and burros in viable free-roaming herds for generations to come, as part of our national heritage.

The AWHPC is a broad-based coalition of more than 50 public interest groups, environmentalists, humane organizations and historical societies representing over 10 million supporters. A campaign, as opposed to a stand alone organization, the AWHPC operates under the 501C3 structure of Return to Freedom, which is its parent organization. http://wildhorsepreservation.org/

The Wild Horse Conspiracy by Craig C. Downer
This is the very best book I've ever read on the history, science, and plight of America's Wild Horses. I wish everyone in the country would read it!
http://www.amazon.com/Wild-Horse-Conspiracy-Craig-Down-er/dp/1461068983/ref=sr_1_1?ie=UTF8&qid=1378307193&sr=8-1&keywords=the+wild+horse+conspiracy

There are numerous additional books and non-profit organizations, most of whom all pull together when bad things happen. Just Google *wild horse advocates* and join the fight.

For more (and more and more) wild horse videos Google
wild horse videos on You Tube.

The Wild Free Roaming Horse and Burro Act of 1971

In 1971, both houses of Congress passed this law unanimously. Virtually from the day it was passed the BLM and the USFS have ignored and violated the will of the Congress and the law. The BLM has actually and arrogantly stated in court that they have full discretion as to how the law is enforced. Federal Judge Rosemary M. Collyer pointedly corrected the BLM in her ruling against them in the Colorado Wild Hose and Burro Coalition lawsuit telling them in the strongest of words that any discretionary powers are specifically for the purpose of management and protection of the wild horses and burros and specifically subject to and in accordance with the provisions of the law. The BLM did not appeal. Links to more on this law follow:

The text of the entire 1971 law:

http://www.wildhorseandburro.blm.gov/92-195.htm

Our beliefs regarding how to win this battle and save the wild horses:

http://thesoulofahorse.com/blog/how-to-save-americas-wild-horses/

Analysis of the key language in the law and how the BLM is violating that language:

http://thesoulofahorse.com/analysis-of-key-language-of-the-wild-free-roaming-horses-and-burros-act-of-1971/

Indigenous Species

The clear and concise proof that the wild horses
of the American west are very definitely an
indigenous native species and not merely
feral escaped domestic livestock as claimed
by cattle and sheep ranchers:

http://thesoulofahorse.com/articles-by-joe/wild-horses-very-definitely-an-indigenous-native-species-in-the-western-united-states/

How Domestic Horses Can Live the Wild Horse Lifestyle

Articles & Blog Links

The Wild Horse Model
http://thesoulofahorse.com/blog/why-the-wild-horse-model/

Our Paddocks Paradise
http://thesoulofahorse.com/blog/our-paddocks-paradise-2/

Meet Happier Healthier Horses Around the World
http://thesoulofahorse.com/blog/powerful-stories-from-happier-healthier-horses/

Why Are These Horses Eating Hay?
http://thesoulofahorse.com/blog/why-are-these-horses-eating-hay/

Five Undeniable Truths About Horses
http://thesoulofahorse.com/blog/why-the-wild-horse-model/five-undeniable-truths-about-horses/

Diet & Nutrition
http://thesoulofahorse.com/blog/diet-nutrition/

How Domestic Horses Can Live the Wild Horse Lifestyle

Books

The Soul of a Horse
Life Lessons from the Herd
http://thesoulofahorse.com/blog/the-books-of-joe-camp/the-soul-of-a-horse-life-lessons-from-the-herd/

Horses & Stress
Eliminating the Root Cause of Most Health,
Hoof & Behavior Problems
http://thesoulofahorse.com/blog/the-books-of-joe-camp/horses-stress/

Horses Were Born to Be On Grass
How We Discovered the Simple But Undeniable Truth
About Grass, Sugar, Equine Diet & Lifestyle
http://thesoulofahorse.com/blog/the-books-of-joe-camp/ebook-nuggets-from-the-soul-of-a-horse-2/horses-were-born-to-be-on-grass/

Horses Without Grass
How We Kept Six Horses Moving and
Eating Happily, Healthily on an Acre and a Half
of Rock and Dirt

http://thesoulofahorse.com/blog/the-books-of-joe-camp/ebook-nuggets-from-the-soul-of-a-horse-2/horses-without-grass/

Why Our Horses Are Barefoot
Everything We've Learned About the Health
and Happiness of the Hoof
http://thesoulofahorse.com/blog/the-books-of-joe-camp/ebook-nuggets-from-the-soul-of-a-horse-2/why-our-horses-are-barefoot-2/

The Soul of a Horse Blogged
The Journey Continues
(Part Two of this book)
http://thesoulofahorse.com/blog/the-books-of-joe-camp/the-soul-of-a-horse-blogged-the-journey-continues/

How Domestic Horses Can Live the Wild Horse Lifestyle Video

Our Paddock Paradise: What We Did,
How We Did It, and Why
http://www.youtube.com/watch?v=bTI4afF3JA8&list=TL8Kjcd0Y83Nw

About Barefoot

Taking your horses barefoot involves more than just pulling shoes. The best of the new breed of natural hoof care practitioners have studied and rely completely on what they call the **wild horse model,** which replicates the trim that horses give to themselves in the wild through natural wear. The more the domesticated horse is out and about, moving constantly, the less trimming he or she will need. The more stall-bound the horse, the more trimming will be needed in order to keep the hooves healthy and in shape. Every horse is a candidate to live as nature intended. The object is to maintain their hooves as if they were in the wild, and that requires some study. Not a lot, but definitely some. I now consider myself capable of keeping my horses' hooves in shape over a short period of time. I don't do their regular trim, but I do perform interim touch-ups. I prefer to have someone who sees hundreds of horses' hooves every week. The myth that domesticated horses *must* wear shoes has been proven to be pure hogwash. The fact that shoes degenerate the health of the hoof and the entire horse has not only been proven, but is also recognized even by many of those who nail shoes on horses. Successful high performance barefootedness with the wild horse trim can be accomplished for virtually every horse on the planet, and the process has even been proven to be a healing procedure for horses with laminitis, founder, navicular, etc. On this subject, I beg you not to wait. Dive into the material below and give your horse a longer, healthier, happier life.

About Barefoot - Articles

Why Barefoot?
http://thesoulofahorse.com/why-barefoot/

Five Undeniable Truths About Horses
http://thesoulofahorse.com/blog/why-the-wild-horse-model/five-undeniable-truths-about-horses/

The Houston Mounted Police Patrol
All Barefoot
http://thesoulofahorse.com/city-of-houston-police-horses-all-barefoot/

Meet Happier Healthier Horses Around the World
http://thesoulofahorse.com/blog/powerful-stories-from-happier-healthier-horses/

About Barefoot - Books

Horses & Stress – Eliminating the Root Cause of Most Health, Hoof & Behavior Problems
http://thesoulofahorse.com/blog/the-books-of-joe-camp/horses-stress/

Why Our Horses Are Barefoot
Everything We've Learned About the Health
and Happiness of the Hoof
http://thesoulofahorse.com/blog/the-books-of-joe-
camp/ebook-nuggets-from-the-soul-of-a-horse-2/why-our-
horses-are-barefoot-2/

The Soul of a Horse
Life Lessons from the Herd
http://thesoulofahorse.com/blog/the-books-of-joe-
camp/the-soul-of-a-horse-life-lessons-from-the-herd/

About Barefoot – Videos

Why Are Our Horses Barefoot?
http://www.youtube.com/watch?v=V2ZofRxB1bU&list=P
L5ED6DAE86CFD04FE&index=10

Our Paddock Paradise: What We Did,
How We Did It, and Why
http://www.youtube.com/watch?v=bTI4afF3JA8&list=TL8
Kjcd0Y83Nw

Why Our Horses Eat from the Ground
http://www.youtube.com/watch?v=g1Gxkpr1hPo&list=PL
5ED6DAE86CFD04FE

The next two videos at the are very short slow-motion videos
of a horse's hoof hitting the ground. One is a shod hoof, one

is barefoot. Watch the vibrations roll up the leg from the shod hoof... then imagine that happening every time any shod hoof hits the ground. Go to:

Trotting Shod Hoof
http://www.youtube.com/watch?v=fql-xsofeg0&list=PL5ED6DAE86CFD04FE

Trotting Barefoot Hoof
http://www.youtube.com/watch?v=_6yLEdr2EOM&list=PL5ED6DAE86CFD04FE&index=20

About Barefoot - Websites

http://www.hoofrehab.com/

This is Pete Ramey's website. If you read only one book on this entire subject, read Pete's *Making Natural Hoof Care Work for You*. Or better yet, get his DVD series *Under the Horse*, which is fourteen-plus hours of terrific research, trimming, and information. If you've ever doubted the fact that horses do not need metal shoes and are in fact better off without them, please go to Pete's website. He will convince you otherwise. Then use his teachings to guide your horses' venture into barefootedness. He is never afraid or embarrassed to change his opinion on something as he learns more from his experiences. Pete's writings have also appeared in *Horse & Rider* and are on his website. He has taken all of Clinton Anderson's horses barefoot.

https://www.facebook.com/pages/Drabek-Natural-Hoof-Care/152654268160182 This is the Facebook site of Eddie Drabek, (Drabek Natural Hoof Care) another one of my heroes. Eddie is a wonderful trimmer in Houston, Texas, and an articulate and inspirational educator and spokesman for getting metal shoes off horses. Read everything he or Tiffany have written, including the pieces on all the horses whose lives he has saved by taking them barefoot.

http://www.thehorseshoof.com/
This website and magazine of Yvonne and James Welz is devoted entirely to barefoot horses around the world and is surely the single largest resource for owners, trimmers, case histories, and virtually everything you would ever want to know about barefoot horses. With years and years of barefoot experience, Yvonne is an amazing resource. She can compare intelligently this method vs that and help you to understand all there is to know. And James is a super barefoot trimmer.

http://www.barefoothorsetrimming.com/
Our current hoof specialist in Tennessee is Mark Taylor who works in Tennessee, Arkansas, Alabama, and Mississippi 662-224-4158

http://www.aanhcp.net
This is the website for the American Association of Natural Hoof Care Practioners.

Find a recommended trimmer in your area at one of these links:

http://www.liberatedhorsemanship.com/Liberated_Horsemanship_Home.html

http://www.aanhcp.net/

http://www.americanhoofassociation.org/

http://www.pacifichoofcare.org/

Relationship & Training

There are, I'm certain, many programs and people who subscribe to these philosophies and are very good at what they do but are not listed in these resources. That's because we haven't experienced them, and we will only recommend to you programs that we believe, from our own personal experience, to be good for the horse and well worth the time and/or money. First I've listed a few links from our website and blog that relate to this subject:

Relationship & Training
Videos

Joe and Cash: Relationship First!
http://www.youtube.com/watch?v=6LqaPdkhS-s&feature=c4-overview-vl&list=PL5ED6DAE86CFD04FE

Finding The Soul of a Horse
http://www.youtube.com/watch?v=zL4jA9Kgmgw&feature=
c4-overview-vl&list=PL5ED6DAE86CFD04FE

Don't Ask for Patience – God
Will Give You a Horse
http://www.youtube.com/watch?v=uBVfvvdfgLo&list=PL5
ED6DAE86CFD04FE

Relationship & Training
Books

The Soul of a Horse
Life Lessons from the Herd
http://thesoulofahorse.com/blog/the-books-of-joe-
camp/the-soul-of-a-horse-life-lessons-from-the-herd/

Why Relationship First Works
Why and How It Changes Everything
http://thesoulofahorse.com/blog/the-books-of-joe-
camp/ebook-nuggets-from-the-soul-of-a-horse-2/why-
relationship-first-works/

Beginning Ground Work
Everything We've Learned About Relationship and Leadership
http://thesoulofahorse.com/blog/the-books-of-joe-
camp/ebook-nuggets-from-the-soul-of-a-horse-
2/beginning-ground-work/

Training with Treats
With Relationship and Basic Training Locked In
Treats Can Be a Way to Enhance Good Communication
http://thesoulofahorse.com/blog/the-books-of-joe-camp/ebook-nuggets-from-the-soul-of-a-horse-2/trainingh-with-treats/

Horses & Stress – Eliminating the Root Cause of Most Health, Hoof & Behavior Problems
http://thesoulofahorse.com/blog/the-books-of-joe-camp/horses-stress/

Relationship & Training
Articles & Posts

Everything Changes When Relationship is First
http://thesoulofahorse.com/before-everything/

Leadership Second
http://thesoulofahorse.com/blog/what-is-leadership/

What's In It for the Horse?
http://thesoulofahorse.com/blog/whats-in-it-for-the-horse/
No Agenda Time

Relationship & Training
Websites

Natural Horsemanship is the current buzz word for those who train horses or teach humans the training of horses without any use of fear, cruelty, threats, aggression, or pain. The philosophy is growing like wildfire, and why shouldn't it? If you can accomplish everything you could ever hope for with your horse and still have a terrific relationship with him or her, and be respected as a leader, not feared as a dominant predator, why wouldn't you? As with any broadly based general philosophy, there are many differing schools of thought on what is important and what isn't, what works well and what doesn't. Which of these works best for you, I believe, depends a great deal on how you learn, and how much reinforcement and structure you need. Our beginning is more or less a shuffling together of the first three below whose websites are listed, favoring one source for this and another for that. Often, this gives us an opportunity to see how different programs handle the same topic, which enriches insight. But, ultimately, they all end up at the same place: When you have a good relationship with your horse that began with the horse's choice, when you are respected as your horse's leader, when you truly care for your horse, then, before too long, you will be able to figure out for yourself the best communication to evoke any particular objective. These programs, as written, or taped on DVD, merely give you a structured format to follow that will take you to that goal.

Monty Roberts and Join up:

http://www.montyroberts.com

Start here, please. Or at Monty's Equus Online University which is terrific and probably the best Equine learning value out there on the internet. Learn Monty's Join-Up method. Watching his *Join-Up* DVD was probably our single most pivotal experience. Even if you've owned your horse forever, go back to the beginning and watch this DVD (or watch Join-Up at his Online University), then do it yourself with your horse or horses. You'll find that when you unconditionally offer choice to your horse and he chooses you, everything changes. You become a member of the herd, and your horse's leader, and with that goes responsibility on his part as well as yours. Even if you don't own horses, it is absolutely fascinating to watch Monty put a saddle and a rider on a completely unbroken horse in less than thirty minutes (unedited!). In the beginning we also watched and used Monty's *Dually Training Halter* DVD and his *Load-Up trailering* DVD. And we loved his books: *The Man Who Listens to Horses, The Horses in My Life, From My Hands to Yours, and Shy Boy.* Monty is a very impressive man who cares a great deal for horses.

http://www.parelli.com

Pat and Linda Parelli have turned their teaching methods into a fully accredited college curriculum. We have four of their home DVD courses: *Level 1, Level 2, Level 3,* and *Liberty & Horse Behavior.* We recommend them all, but especially the first three. Often, they do run on, dragging out points much longer than perhaps necessary, but we've found, particularly in the early days, that knowledge gained through such saturation always bubbles up to present itself at the most opportune moments. In other words, it's good. Soak it up. It'll pay dividends later. Linda is a good instructor, especially in the first three programs, and Pat is one of the most amazing horsemen I've ever seen. His antics are inspirational for me. Not that I will ever duplicate many of them, but knowing that it's possible is very affirming. Pat's 17-minute demonstration teaching Games 2, 3, and 4 to a new untrained horse on DVD #2 of their Level 1 Kit was worth the price of the entire set. Virtually everything you need to know about groundwork is in that 17 minutes. Soak this man up anytime you can. And watching him with a newborn foal is just fantastic. The difficulty for us with *Liberty & Horse Behavior* (besides its price) is on disk 5 whereon Linda consumes almost three hours to load an inconsistent horse into a trailer. Her belief is that the horse should *not* be *made* to do anything, he should *discover* it on his own. I believe there's another option. As Monty Roberts teaches, there is a big difference between *making* a horse do something and *leading* him through it, showing him that it's okay, that his trust in you is valid. Once you have joined up with him, and he trusts you, he is willing to take chances for you because of that trust, so long as you don't abuse the trust. On Monty's trailer-loading DVD Monty takes about one-tenth the time, and the horse (who was impossible to load before Monty) winds up loading himself from thirty feet away, happily, even playfully. And his trust in Monty has progressed as well, because he reached beyond his comfort zone and learned it was okay. His trust was confirmed. And I've never seen Pat

Parelli take longer than maybe 30 minutes to teach a horse to load. One thing the Parelli program stresses, in a way, is a follow up to Monty Roberts' Join-Up: you should spend a lot of time just hanging out with your horse. In the stall, in the pasture, wherever. Quality time, so to speak. No agenda, just hanging out. Very much a relationship enhancer. And don't ever stomp straight over to your horse and slap on a halter. Wait. Let your horse come to you. It's that choice thing again, and Monty or Pat and Linda Parelli can teach you how it works.

http://www.downunderhorsemanship.com

This is Clinton Anderson's site. Whereas the Parellis are very philosophically oriented, Clinton gets down to business with lots of detail and repetition. What exactly do I do to get my horse to back up? From the ground and from the saddle, he shows you precisely, over and over again. And when you're in the arena or round pen and forget whether he used his left hand or right hand, or whether his finger was pointing up or down, it's very easy to go straightaway to the answer on his DVDs. His programs are very task-oriented, and, again, there are a bunch of them. We have consumed his *Gaining Respect and Control on the Ground, Series I through III* and *Riding with Confidence, Series I through III*. And his new *Fundamentals* program. All are multiple DVD sets, so there has been a lot of viewing and reviewing. For the most part, his tasks and the Parellis are much the same, though usually the teaching is approached very differently. Both have served a purpose for us. We also loved his *No Worries Tying DVD* for use with his Australian Tie Ring, which truly eliminates pull-back problems in minutes! And on this one he demonstrates terrific desensitizing techniques. It's sad that Clinton Anderson does not begin with relationship first (except with his own personal horses) but I feel he is one of the best teachers around, especially if you're a 1-2-3 kind of learner. His basic ground work fundamentals are effective, precise, clear, and simple to understand and execute. Clinton is a two-time winner of the Road to the Horse competition, in which three top natural-horsemanship clinicians are given unbroken horses and a mere three hours to be riding and performing specified tasks. Those DVDs are terrific! And Clinton's Australian accent is also fun to listen to... mate.

The three programs above have built our natural horsemanship foundation, and we are in their debt. The following are a few others you should probably check out, each featuring a highly respected clinician, and all well known for their care and concern for horses.

http://www.imagineahorse.com

This is Allen Pogue and Suzanne De Laurentis' site. Allen's work has unfortunately cast him as a trick trainer, but it's so much more than that. We've just recently discovered Allen and are dumbfounded by how his horses treat him and try for him. His work with young horses is so logical and powerful that you should study it even if you never intend to own a horse. Allen says "With my young horses, by the time they are three years old they are so mentally mature that saddling and a short ride is absolutely undramatic." He has taken Dr.

Robert M. Miller's book *Imprint Training of the Newborn Foal* to a new and exponential level.

http://www.robertmmiller.com
Dr. Robert M. Miller is an equine veterinarian and world renowned speaker and author on horse behavior and natural horsemanship. I think his name comes up more often in these circles than anyone else's. His first book, *Imprint Training of the Newborn Foal* is now a bible of the horse world. He's not really a trainer, per se, but a phenomenal resource on horse behavior. He will show you the route to "the bond." You must visit his website.

http://www.chrislombard.com/
An amazing horseman and wonderful teacher. His DVD *Beginning with the Horse* puts relationship, leadership and trust into simple easy-to-understand terms. And only one DVD :) Also read his book *Land of the Horses*. As old as I am, it changed my life and I believe it'll change yours as well.

Frederick Pignon – This man is amazing and has taken relationship and bond with his horses to an astounding new level. Go to this link:
http://www.youtube.com/watch?v=w1YO3j-Zh3g
and watch the video of his show with three beautiful black Lusitano stallions, all at liberty. This show would border on the miraculous if they were all geldings, but they're not. They're stallions. Most of us will never achieve the level of bond Frederick has achieved with his horses but it's inspiring to know that it's possible, and to see what the horse-human

relationship is capable of becoming. Frederick believes in true partnership with his horses, he believes in making every training session fun not work, he encourages the horses to offer their ideas, and he uses treats. And when he begins a performance he says that he never knows exactly where it's going to go. When Kathleen read his book *Gallop to Freedom* her response to me was simply, "Can we just move in with them?"

New resources are regularly updated on our
http://theSoulofaHorse.com
or the blog
http://thesoulofahorse.com/blog

Valuable Links on Diet and Nutrition:

Dr. Juliette Getty's website:
http://gettyequinenutrition.biz/

Dr. Getty's favorite feed/forage testing facility:
Equi-Analytical Labs:
http://www.equi-analytical.com

The Diet page on our website:
http://thesoulofahorse.com/a-slippery-slope/

FIVE UNDENIABLE TRUTHS

One: The first Undeniable Truth – Science tells us that it would take a minimum of 5000 years – probably closer to 10,000 – to even begin to change the base genetics of any species. In other words, no matter what anyone tells you to the contrary, a few hundred years of selective breeding has no effect on base genetics whatsoever or the horse's ability to grow the kind of rock solid foot he was born to have. This is the foundation for all that follows. Everything begins right here. The wild horse in the western high desert of the United States has incredible feet. He must have to escape predators and to search for food and water. If he didn't have incredible feet he'd be extinct. We would have never known him. And the wild horse and the domestic horse of today are genetically exactly the same. The domestic horse's foot is not genetically weak and unhealthy. Not even the oft-claimed Thoroughbred. The conditions under which any horse lives can certainly cause ill health, but the horse's genetics can fix that, given the opportunity.

Two: DNA sequencing was done on bones of horses discovered in the Alaskan permafrost dating 12,000 to 28,000 years old… and this DNA sequencing was compared to DNA sequencing from today's domestic horse… and there was less than 1.2% difference in those 28,000 year old horses and the horse in your back yard. Documented and on record. Confirming, once again, that the base genetics of every horse on the planet are the same. Science confirms for us that every horse on this earth "retains the ability to return successfully to the wild or feral state" – note that they say *successfully* – and that includes growing himself or herself a great foot that would protect this flight animal from predators and give him – or her – the ability to travel 8-20 miles every day of his life.

Three: The horse began and evolved for 50+ million years in and around the Great Basin of the western United States... then he crossed the Bering Straits Land Bridge into Siberia spreading into the rest of the world. Which means that the horse – as we know it today – spent 50+ million years evolving – now please get this because it's important – the horse spent 50+ million years evolving to live in conditions and on terrain like the western high desert of the United States and no horse will ever adapt to the terrain and environment in our new home in middle Tennessee...or at least not for 5000 to 10,000 years... and it is therefore up to us – Kathleen and myself – to do everything within our power to replicate the lifestyle they would be living if they were living in the great basin – which is effectively the lifestyle they were living at our high desert home in southern California before moving to middle Tennessee.

The herd in California

The herd in Tennessee

Four: Undeniable Truth #4 (or perhaps #1): a horse's hoof is supposed to flex with every impact of the ground. Every time it hits the ground it flexes outward – like a toilet plunger – and then snaps back when the hoof comes off the ground. That flexing sucks an enormous amount of blood into the hoof mechanism... keeps it healthy, helps it to grow properly, helps fight off problems... AND all that liquid provides an hydraulic-like shock absorption for the joints, ligaments, and tendons of the leg. Wow... who knew? At one point I remember believing the horse's hoof was just a wad of hard stuff... like one big fingernail. But there's more. When the foot lifts off the ground and the flexed hoof snaps back, the power of that contraction shoves the blood in the hoof capsule back up those long skinny legs, taking strain off the heart. So what happens to all this good stuff when a metal shoe is nailed to the hoof?

Nothing.

No circulation (or substantially reduced circulation)... no shock absorption (in fact if you've ever seen the videos of the vibrations set off up the leg when a metal shoe slams into the ground see link below, it'll freak you out)... and no assistance to the heart in getting that blood back up the leg.

Five: There is no hoof lameness in the wild (the wild of the American west where the horse evolved for 50+ million years; the terrain he is well used to living on). Yet the American Farriers Association reports that 95% of domestic horses have some degree of hoof lameness? Some folks want to say that's because the domestic hoof is inherently weak. But as we've already established, the inherent genetics are the same as the wild horse. The reasons for so much domestic hoof lameness are the metal shoes, diet, lifestyle, stress, and in some cases work load that we have forced upon the horse. In other words: No Stalls, no shoes, no sugar! In simple terms, what all this means is that a horse's entire physiology has been built over millions of years to:

Move a minimum of 8 to 20 miles a day, <u>on bare hooves</u>.

Be with a herd, and thus physically and emotionally safe, unstressed.

Spend 16 to 18 hours a day eating… <u>from the ground</u>, a variety, but mostly grass or grass hay; a continuous uptake in small quantities to suit their small tummies and the function of their hindguts.

Control their own thermoregulatory system, thus controlling their own internal body temperature with no outside assistance, including heat, blankets, and the like.

Stand and walk on firm fresh ground, not in the chemical remnants of their own poop and pee… nor be breathing the fumes of those remnants, plus the excessive carbon dioxide that accumulates inside a closed structure. In other words, no stalls.

Get a certain amount of unstressed REM sleep, which requires them to lie down, which will usually only happen when our in the company of other horses, for guard duty.

WHAT READERS AND CRITICS ARE SAYING ABOUT JOE CAMP

"Joe Camp is a master storyteller." - *THE NEW YORK TIMES*

"Joe Camp is a natural when it comes to understanding how animals tick and a genius at telling us their story. His books are must-reads for those who love animals of any species." - *MONTY ROBERTS, AUTHOR OF NEW YORK TIMES BEST-SELLER THE MAN WHO LISTENS TO HORSES*

"The tightly written, simply designed, and powerfully drawn chapters often read like short stories that flow from the heart. Camp has become something of a master at telling us what can be learned from animals, in this case specifically horses, without making us realize we have been educated, and, that is, perhaps, the mark of a real teacher." - *JACK L. KENNEDY, THE JOPLIN INDEPENDENT*

"One cannot help but be touched by Camp's love and sympathy for animals and by his eloquence on the subject." - *MICHAEL KORDA, THE WASHINGTON POST*

"Joe Camp is a gifted storyteller and the results are magical. Joe entertains, educates and empowers, baring his own soul while articulating keystone principles of a modern revolution in horsemanship." - *RICK LAMB, AUTHOR AND TV/RADIO HOST "THE HORSE SHOW"*

Also by Joe Camp

The National Best Seller
The Soul of a Horse
Life Lessons from the Herd

Horses & Stress
Eliminating the Root Cause of
Most Health, Hoof, and Behavior Problems

The Soul of a Horse Blogged
The Journey Continues

God Only Knows
Can You Trust Him with the Secret?

Dog On It
Everything You Need To Know About Life Is Right There At Your Feet

Why Relationship First Works
Why and How It Changes Everything

Beginning Ground Work
Everything We've Learned About Relationship and Leadership

Training with Treats
With Relationship and Basic Training Locked In
Treats Can Be an Excellent Way to Enhance Good Communication

Why Our Horses Are Barefoot
Everything We've Learned About the
Health and Happiness of the Hoof

Horses Were Born To Be On Grass
How We Discovered the Simple But Undeniable
Truth About Grass, Sugar, Equine Diet & Lifestyle

Horses Without Grass
How We Kept Six Horses Moving and Eating Happily
Healthily on an Acre and a Half of Rocks and Dirt

The Benji Method
Teach Your Dog to Do What Benji Does in the Movies

For more information
please visit one of these websites:

thesoulofahorse.com

thesoulofahorse.com/blog

www.14handspress.com

The Soul of a Horse Page on Facebook
https://www.facebook.com/pages/The-Soul-of-a-
Horse/106606472709815

The Soul of a Horse Channel on YouTube
http://www.youtube.com/user/thesoulofahorse

Joe and The Soul of a Horse on Twitter
https://twitter.com/Joe_camp

All of the videos and links in this book are live links in the eBook editions available at Amazon Kindle, Barnes & Noble Nook, and Apple iBooks, and all photos are in color.

49535956R00165

Made in the USA
Lexington, KY
09 February 2016